SMALLVILLE™

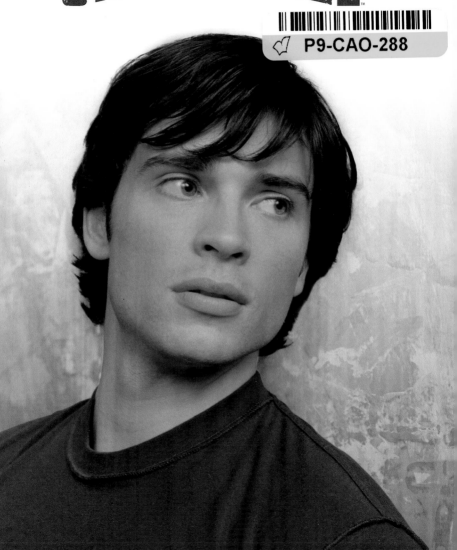

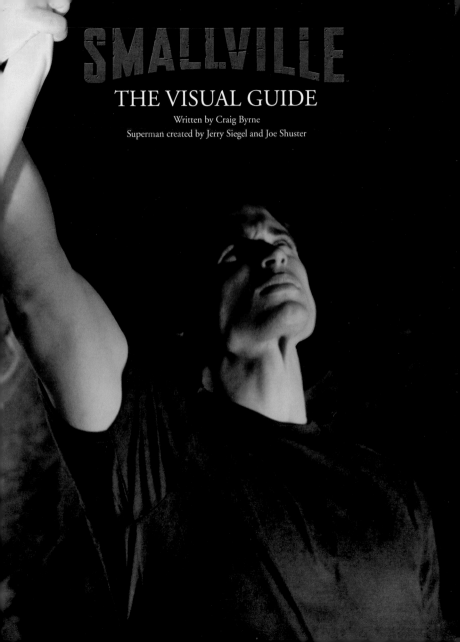

SMALLVILLE

THE VISUAL GUIDE

Written by Craig Byrne

Superman created by Jerry Siegel and Joe Shuster

CONTENTS

Introduction	06-07
Smallville	08-09
The Meteor Shower	10-11
The Kents	12-13
The Kent Farm	14-15
Clark Kent	16-17
Clark's Powers	18-19
Pete Ross	20-21
Chloe Sullivan	22-23
Lana Lang	24-25
The Rescue	26-27
Lex Luthor	28-29
Lionel Luthor	30-31
The Luthors	32-33
The Luthor Mansion	34-35
Mansion Secrets	36-37
Wall of Weird	38-39
More Freaks	40-41
Perry White	42
Mikhail Mxyzptlk	43
Bart "The Flash" Allen	44-45
High School Yearbook	46-47
Kawatche Caves	48-49
Unlocking the Secrets	50-51
Clark's Origins	52-53
Kryptonite	54-55
Kal	56-57
Metropolis	58-59
City Girl	60-61
Lois Lane	62-63
Moving On	64-65
The Teagues	66-67
The Elements	68-69
Fortress of Solitude	70-71
Clark & Lana	72-73
Clark's Fathers	74-75
Martha Kent	76-77
Lex & Clark	78-79
Destiny Calls	80-81
Arthur Curry	82-83
Brainiac	84-85
Lex & Lana	86-87
Developing Powers	88-89
The Future	90-91
Season Six	92-93
The Ultimate Reference	94-95
Acknowledgments	96

FOREWORD

Every legend has a beginning.

For the last five years we have been lucky enough to bring *Smallville* into your homes and recreate the genesis of an American icon. What began with a meteor shower, forever changing a small Kansas town, led to countless twists and turns, including meteor freaks, mysterious ancient caves, spaceships, and a Fortress rising out of the Arctic. Not to mention duplicity, betrayal, friendship, love, and heartache.

We are honored to be able to give something back to the mythos that has meant so much to the believers, dreamers, and the kids in all of us. Superman is a story known to millions, but *Smallville* offers a fresh perspective on the everyday—and the not so everyday—life of that special farm boy on his journey of self-discovery.

While this is the tale of Clark Kent, it is more importantly about foundation. Within these pages you are invited to explore the building blocks of a hero. What gives him strength, such as the wisdom of a beloved departed father. What makes him weak, whether it is a rock from across the universe or the girl from across the way. Most of all, you will recognize what makes him a legend.

Piecing together this visual guide has brought back a lot of memories for us. We hope that you, our companion on this journey, will remember with us, look back with fondness, and look ahead with anticipation.

Enjoy!

Al Gough

Miles Millar

SMALLVILLE

The town of Smallville was formed when fur trader and trapper, Ezra Small, established a trading post alongside the Elbow River in the early 1840s. The post soon grew to consist of several mud and thatch huts, and people began referring to it as "Smallville." The name stuck, and even more people settled into the area. So far Smallville has had the Civil War, tornadoes, and at least two huge meteor showers.

Before the meteor shower in 1989, Smallville was more famous for being the "Creamed Corn Capital of the World." Nowadays it is also famous for its unusual inhabitants and occurrences.

SMALLVILLE HIGH

Smallville High School services grades 9 through 12. The current school building was erected in 1979. The school boasts many extracurricular activities, including a victorious football team and their award-winning student newspaper, *The Torch*.

Smallville High is home to the highly-successful Crows football team, and many of its star players go on to play college football.

LAW AND ORDER

Sheriff Ethan Miller served Smallville until his disdain for Lionel Luthor got the better of him and he attempted to take Luthor's life. Ethan, a classmate of Jonathan Kent, was replaced by no-nonsense Sheriff Nancy Adams from Wichita.

Sheriff Adams didn't buy Clark's excuses as to why he always happened to be at the scene whenever there was trouble.

Crater Lake is a popular hangout for Smallville teens. In summer, the water is unusually warm for the middle of Kansas. Some people believe that the tranquillity of Crater Lake is somehow linked to the green meteor rocks.

HENRY SMALL

Lana's father Henry Small is a descendant of Ezra Small. He is a prominent lawyer, dedicated to environmental concerns. He lives on Maple Street with his wife, Jennifer, and their children, and is highly critical of the Luthors' influence on the town his ancestors helped to create.

EZRA SMALL'S HOUSE

The original home of Ezra Small has been preserved. The main part of the house has been renovated to become the Ezra Small Museum, complete with documents and artifacts celebrating Smallville's rich and unique history.

Dedicated Smallville patriot and idealist Tim Westcott proudly shows Lois Lane a model of pre-meteor shower Smallville at the Ezra Small Museum.

THE TALON

The Talon movie theater first opened in 1939 with a matinée screening of *The Wizard Of Oz*. More than sixty years later, the Talon was purchased by Lex Luthor, who, with Lana Lang, transformed it into a coffee house and popular teen hangout.

THE FERTILIZER PLANT

LuthorCorp Fertilizer Plant No. 3 opened in 1990 after Lionel Luthor purchased the Ross creamed corn factory. At its peak, it was the leading employer in Lowell County.

HALF PRICE
LATTES
ALL WEEK

SMALLVILLE MEDICAL CENTER

The Smallville Medical Center employs some of the best doctors in the country and boasts state-of-the-art facilities—which are often called into emergency use due to the special abilities of some Smallville residents.

THE METEOR SHOWER

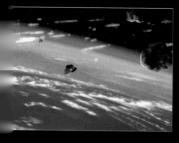

October 16, 1989 started out the same as any other day in Smallville. Jonathan and Martha Kent headed into town to pick up supplies, Nell Potter babysat her young niece Lana while her parents ran some errands in Metropolis, the Smallville High football jocks selected and hung their first Scarecrow, and Lionel Luthor was about to close a deal that would give him ownership of the town's largest business. Then, seemingly out of nowhere, a massive meteor shower hit. Huge fireballs rained down from the sky so quickly that many people found it impossible to escape them.

FAMILY TRAGEDY

Lewis and Laura Lang had just arrived in town to pick up their young daughter Lana from her aunt Nell, when the meteors hit. Across the street, little Lana's excitement turned to horror as she witnessed the meteor shower claim the lives of her beloved parents, in an instant.

Flames engulfed many buildings.

KANSAS TOWN DEVASTATED

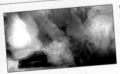

Yesterday the picturesque Kansas town of Smallville became the unlikely meteor capital of the world.

Reports claim that more than four dozen people were injured and ten people died in the meteor blasts. Information at this time is sketchy, although we can confirm that Alexander Luthor, son of Metropolis fertilizer mogul Lionel Luthor, was among those admitted to the Smallville Medical Center. The famed Smallville water tower and the Smallville Grand Hotel were also destroyed by the falling meteors.

Those interested in contributing to relief efforts should attend a special town meeting in the Smallville High School auditorium.

"Today was a dark day for Smallville, and it will be weeks before we can completely rebuild."

Sheriff Waid

A memorial service for those who lost their lives will follow in due course.

METEOR FACTS

• The meteor shower left fragments of green rocks all around Smallville. The strange rocks emitted a radioactive energy that caused mutations in some of the people that came into contact with them.

• Although cleanup crews were brought in to clear the area, rocks have been found up to ten years later in abandoned buildings such as the Smallville Foundry.

• People began experiencing physical changes soon after exposure to the rocks. Cassandra Carver went blind, Lex Luthor went bald, and Tina Greer's incurable soft bone disease was miraculously cured.

AMAZING JOURNEY

The meteors were not the only thing heading for Smallville on that day. A Kryptonian ship containing baby Kal-El, the Last Son of Krypton, traveled past several galaxies and light years to get to its final destination. The ship was powered by a special vortex engine created by Kal-El's father, Jor-El.

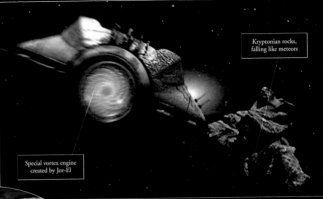

Kryptonian rocks, falling like meteors

Special vortex engine created by Jor-El

Although happily married, the Kents were unable to have children. After meeting cute little Lana Lang in Nell Potter's flower shop, Martha Kent's longing for child of her own intensified.

Caught up in the meteor shower, the Kents attempted to outrun the falling rocks as they sped along Route 40. They weren't fast enough, and ended up being thrown off the road.

PRAYERS ANSWERED

As the Kents emerged from their toppled truck, they were greeted by the unexpected sight of a smiling young boy whose nearby spaceship indicated that he probably wasn't from Kansas. To Martha it seemed that amongst the devastation, her wish for a child had come true at last.

THE KENTS

The Kents were devastated that they could not have children, but the meteor shower provided a surprising addition to their family.

TOUGH TIMES

The Kent farm has been through some tough financial times, and the Kents often struggle to make ends meet. But stubborn Jonathan is too proud to accept money from Martha's wealthy father or people like the Luthors.

Sophisticated and privileged Martha Clark met her future husband while studying law at Metropolis University. Jonathan Kent, a handsome young farmer, was taking a break from his finance course when Martha, looking for an excuse to talk to him, asked if she could borrow his class notes. Jonathan immediately handed them over without question, prompting Martha to ask how she knew she would give them back. When Jonathan replied, "I prefer to believe in people," Martha was immediately smitten.

Martha's father wasn't too happy with his daughter's decision to drop everything and marry a farmer, but Martha has always been a strong-willed woman. Later on she went to work for Lionel Luthor, despite her husband's protests. Although Martha holds a soft spot for Lionel, her heart will always belong to her husband.

A REGULAR FAMILY

Clark has grown up as part of a loving and supportive family. The Kents pride themselves on old-fashioned values such as honesty, respect, loyalty, and a hearty family breakfast every morning. Jonathan and Martha Kent are the only parents Clark has ever really known and, regardless of his biological origins, Clark truly feels like their son.

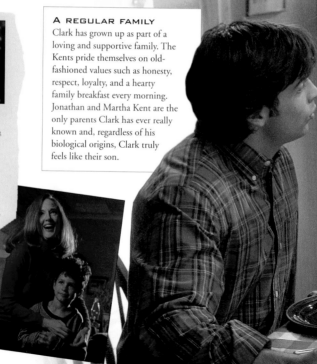

After the 1989 meteor shower, Sheriff Ethan Miller visited the Kents to check that they were safe. When the sheriff saw the child, Martha introduced him as their adopted son, whom they had just picked up from Metropolis. Thinking quickly, she gave the boy her family name.

• The Kents kept Clark's ship in the storm cellar and didn't tell him about it until he was old enough to understand.

• Jonathan Kent's father didn't tell his son that he had cancer until two weeks before he died. Jonathan promised himself that he would never keep secrets from his son.

• Martha Kent remained estranged from her father after her marriage because she couldn't risk him discovering Clark's special abilities.

...though they are reluctant to ...courage their son to ...ter a dangerous ...uation, the ...nts have ...ways taught ...m to do ... right ...ng.

Martha puts her family above everything else.

When Jonathan and Martha Kent chaperoned the Smallville High School senior Prom, they couldn't help but feel proud of their amazing son.

Plaid is a popular part of the Kent family wardrobe.

THE KENT FARM

The Kent farm is located on Hickory Lane just outside the town of Smallville, on Rural Route 8.

Clark is the fourth generation of the Kent family to live on the farm. In 1871, Sheriff Nathaniel Kent and his wife bought the land and built a two-room timber farm house. Then, in 1903, they built a larger home, closer to the dirt road that led into town. In 1957, Hiram Kent added a second story to his father's house, and when Hiram's son Jonathan took over the farm with his new wife Martha, he added a wraparound porch. The Kent farm has survived the 1930's Dust Bowl, tornadoes, snowstorms, two meteor showers, and more than one major explosion.

After a direct hit from the second meteor shower, the Kent's farmhouse was rebuilt and restored to its original glory.

FARM AT WORK

The Kents keep cows and chickens and also grow organic fruit. Most weeks, they sell their produce at the farmers' market in Smallville. At one time the farm employed about a dozen workers, but these days the Kents are lucky enough to have a very gifted son to help with the chores!

STARGAZING

The Kent farm offers
unparalleled views of the night
sky. Clark spends a lot of his free
time in the barn, looking
through his telescope at faraway
places. At one time, the telescope
also offered him an advantageous
view of the Kents' next door
neighbors, Nell Potter and her
teenage niece, Lana Lang.

Jonathan Kent also keeps his farming
equipment in the barn. Clark spends so
much time in the loft there that Jonathan
calls it his "Fortress of Solitude."

CLARK KENT

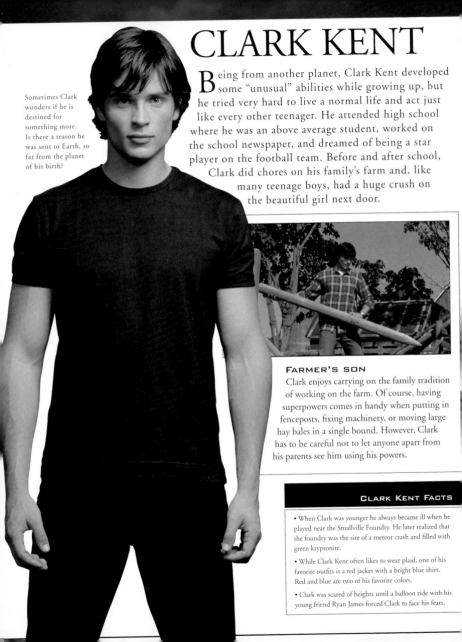

Sometimes Clark wonders if he is destined for something more. Is there a reason he was sent to Earth, so far from the planet of his birth?

Being from another planet, Clark Kent developed some "unusual" abilities while growing up, but he tried very hard to live a normal life and act just like every other teenager. He attended high school where he was an above average student, worked on the school newspaper, and dreamed of being a star player on the football team. Before and after school, Clark did chores on his family's farm and, like many teenage boys, had a huge crush on the beautiful girl next door.

FARMER'S SON

Clark enjoys carrying on the family tradition of working on the farm. Of course, having superpowers comes in handy when putting in fenceposts, fixing machinery, or moving large hay bales in a single bound. However, Clark has to be careful not to let anyone apart from his parents see him using his powers.

CLARK KENT FACTS

- When Clark was younger he always became ill when he played near the Smallville Foundry. He later realized that the foundry was the site of a meteor crash and filled with green kryptonite.

- While Clark Kent often likes to wear plaid, one of his favorite outfits is a red jacket with a bright blue shirt. Red and blue are two of his favorite colors.

- Clark was scared of heights until a balloon ride with his young friend Ryan James forced Clark to face his fears.

When not hanging out with his two best friends, Pete Ross and Chloe Sullivan, or working on the *Torch* newspaper, Clark studied hard and was determined to make his parents proud. His favorite classes were English, science, and gym.

Clark always seemed to make a fool of himself when he was around Lana Lang. Chloe joked that "Clark Kent can't get within five feet of Lana Lang without turning into a total freak show." However, Clark later realized that it was more than just being around a girl he likes—the real reason was the meteor rock necklace Lana wore in memory of her dead parents.

LOCAL BOY IS A HERO!

Smallville High's star quarterback, Whitney Fordman, was injured yesterday when his pickup truck spun out of control and flipped onto its side on Cryzis Road. Fortunately for the Smallville High Crows football team and their coach Walt Arnold, Fordman was released from the Smallville Medical Center with only minor injuries. Fordman insists that the accident was caused by someone or something on top of his roof, but his allegation cannot be confirmed at this time. Local farmer's son Clark Kent was near the scene of the accident. Kent was able to pull Fordman to safety, while avoiding the fire and miraculously escaping injury.

"I don't know how he did it."

Fire Marshal Bill Tyler

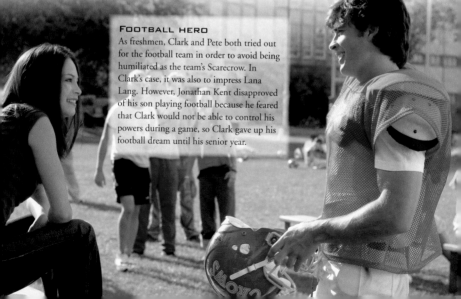

FOOTBALL HERO

As freshmen, Clark and Pete both tried out for the football team in order to avoid being humiliated as the team's Scarecrow. In Clark's case, it was also to impress Lana Lang. However, Jonathan Kent disapproved of his son playing football because he feared that Clark would not be able to control his powers during a game, so Clark gave up his football dream until his senior year.

CLARK'S POWERS

Adolescence brings changes in any young man's body, but coming of age when you're from Krypton is a totally different story. As Clark got older, he realized that he can do things that his friends cannot. Sometimes those powers were beneficial, giving Clark the ability to help those he loves, but at other times the burden of concealing them from nearly everyone weighed heavily on his shoulders. Although his parents offered him unlimited love and support, they too had no idea what their son might be capable of.

When Clark first discovered that he had heat vision, he used it to make everyday things easier, such as making toast. However, he has learned to focus this power so he can project heat in any direction.

SUPERSPEED

Clark Kent discovered that he could run extraordinarily fast at the age of six. While playing a game of tag with his father, he started running so fast that he ended up lost and frightened, several miles away in Palmer Woods. As Clark has grown older his speed has increased even further, and he can now run faster than a speeding bullet!

STRONG AS STEEL

Clark seems to be invulnerable. As long as there are no meteor rocks around, he can withstand extreme force and intense heat. Clark also has superstrength, which comes in very handy around the farm because he can do the work of several laborers, in half the time.

To prove his invulnerability, Clark put his hand in a wood chipper. He emerged with only a torn shirt!

Clark's powers come from exposure to the rays of Earth's yellow sun. His Kryptonian body cells store the sun's energy like a solar battery. Once, when a comet collided with the sun, the solar flares caused Clark's powers to malfunction. Without warning, Clark found his powers disappearing and then amplifying, with embarassing consequences. Without the sun, Clark would have no superpowers.

X-RAY VISION

Clark's X-ray vision allows him to see through walls and has also assisted him in locating kidnapped friends. He used this power to track shapeshifter Tina Greer as she morphed into new forms. However, just like regular X-rays, Clark cannot see through lead.

When Clark first discovered this power, it appeared unexpectedly, giving him a sneaky peek at the girl's locker room during gym class!

CLARK'S WEAKNESS

Besides Lana Lang, Clark has one major weakness—the meteor rocks that fell on Smallville the day he arrived on Earth. These glowing green rocks from the planet Krypton are known as "kryptonite," and cause Clark to become sick and lose his powers. Prolonged exposure to kryptonite would eventually kill him. When Whitney Fordman and the other football players hung Clark up as that year's Scarecrow, wearing Lana's necklace, Clark was rendered powerless. Fortunately, Lex Luthor eventually rescued him.

A meteor rock can render Clark powerless and help a villain to escape. Thankfully, not many people are aware of Clark's weakness.

PETE ROSS

Pete Ross and Clark Kent became good friends in elementary school when Clark fought back against a school bully. Though Clark used a little bit of superstrength against the bully, sending him through a door, Pete didn't suspect that his best friend was anything more than a regular guy. Years later, Pete became Clark's first friend to learn the truth about him.

In 1989, Lionel Luthor bought the creamed corn factory from the Ross family. He promised them that no changes would be made to their factory, but as soon as the deal was signed, Lionel laid off the entire staff. Many families in Smallville suffered as a result, and the Rosses felt betrayed by Lionel Luthor.

ONE OF THE GOOD GUYS

Pete Ross' life changed irrevocably when he came across Clark's spaceship in a cornfield. Clark decided to share his secret with his friend and, aside from some near-accidents, Pete kept Clark's secret and refused to give him up. However, the burden of Clark's secret took its toll on Pete, and in the future Clark will think long and hard before confiding in another friend.

When Pete and Clark's friendship went through a rough time, Pete took up drag racing. But, when the situation got dangerous, Pete turned to Clark for help.

SECRET FEELINGS

Though he thought that his feelings were well hidden, most people knew that Pete had a big crush on his friend Chloe Sullivan. Unfortunately for Pete, Chloe was far more interested in Clark, and Pete's feelings were to remain unrequited.

Pete only declared his true feelings when Chloe was affected by a meteor spray that made others tell the truth.

LOCAL KID ATTACKS LUTHOR

Smallville resident and billionaire Lex Luthor very nearly paid with his life for the sins of his father when he was attacked by a local boy yesterday in his own home.

Pete Ross, 16, member of a prominent Smallville family that can be traced back five generations, is believed to have threatened Mr. Luthor with a gun.

It is thought that the attack was motivated by bad feeling following the closing of the Ross creamed corn factory in 1989.

This newspaper can exclusively reveal that Ross was affected with the same condition that struck down three other

Smallville residents this week. Unconfirmed sources claim the condition is due to a rare "Nicodemus flower" which causes an allergic reaction in its victims and makes them behave completely out of character.

Pete Ross is currently in Smallville Medical Center, but is expected to make a full recovery. Lex Luthor was unharmed and has decided not to press charges against his attacker.

BEST BUDDIES

Every hero needs a sidekick, and for many years Pete Ross and Clark Kent were best friends. In Pete, Clark had a buddy who knew all his secrets—his unusual origins, his amazing powers, and his feelings for Lana Lang.

Pete understood the serious stuff in Clark's life, but he was also there for the normal teenage things such as checking out cute girls!

PETE ROSS FACTS

• Pete is the youngest of five overachieving siblings: Sam "Deuce" Ross was a star player for the Smallville Crows football team, Mike excelled in science courses, Mark became a successful businessman in Topeka, and sister Kathy was class valedictorian. Pete feels he has a lot to live up to.

• Pete's mother is the Honorable Judge Abigail Ross, who transferred to Wichita after separating from her husband.

TOUGH GOODBYE

The pressures and dangers of knowing Clark's secret became too much for Pete to handle, so when his mother got a new job in Wichita, he decided to leave Smallville and go with her.

CHLOE SULLIVAN

Lana and Chloe weren't always close—their feelings for Clark were an issue—but they overcame their differences to become good friends. When Lana's aunt Nell moved to Metropolis, Chloe offered Lana a place to stay so she could remain in Smallville.

A girl with a nose for news, like Chloe Sullivan, was never going to take the weird happenings in Smallville lightly. In fact, she was one of the first people to come up with the theory that meteor rocks caused freakish behavior, and collected data for her "Wall of Weird." At first Chloe's theories were often not taken seriously, but as the meteor-linked happenings became more frequent, it was clear that Chloe was on to something big.

While cute Tyler Randall dated Chloe, his bio-duplicate was seeing Lana Lang at the same time!

BOY TROUBLE

For such a smart girl and expert on meteor freaks, Chloe has made some poor choices of boyfriends. Ice-cool Sean Kelvin, two-faced Tyler Randall, jinxy Mikhail Mxyzptlk, and telekinetic Justin Gaines all made her wish for a nice regular guy. Like Clark Kent, for example...

CHLOE FACTS

• Chloe was born in Metropolis. She and her father Gabe moved to Smallville when he was assigned to the Luthor fertilizer plant.

• Chloe's mother left the family when Chloe was just five years old. Mrs. Sullivan was institutionalized when Chloe was 12.

• Chloe received her first byline in the *Smallville Ledger* when her *Torch* article about "superboy" Eric Summers was picked up by the paper.

• Chloe spent the summer after her freshman year as an intern at the *Daily Planet* newspaper.

SIEGE AT LUTHOR PLANT

A desperate lone gunman took over the LuthorCorp fertilizer plant and held several Smallville High School students, their teacher, and plant manager Gabe Sullivan hostage. After four tense hours, the intruder released all hostages and surrendered to police.

Former plant employee Earl Jenkins is wanted for the murder of a LuthorCorp Tower janitor. Jenkins, who gained access to the LuthorCorp building by overpowering a security guard and stealing his uniform, claims to have been poisoned after working in a "secret" area called "Level Three," and returned to the plant to confront Lionel Luthor. Jenkins was brought out peacefully and taken to Smallville Medical Center, along with Smallville High football star Whitney Fordman.

SUFFERING FOR A STORY

A visit to the Luthor mansion for an exclusive interview found Chloe in the wrong place at the wrong time as thieves sent her flying out of an upper-story window. It certainly wouldn't be the only time that Chloe's pursuit of a story would put her into a dangerous situation.

Chloe often felt that Clark was too distant, until she became aware of the secrets that burden him. Meanwhile, Clark does his best to ignore Chloe's romantic feelings for him and they manage to maintain a very close friendship.

PUSHING TOO HARD

Chloe's interest in the mysteries surrounding her friend Clark Kent often led to awkward and uncomfortable situations. Clark reacted particularly badly when Chloe looked into finding his "real" parents.

THE *TORCH*

Chloe spent her high school years as editor of the Smallville High student newspaper, the *Torch*. 1000 copies of each issue were printed and distributed free to students. The *Torch* provided Chloe with an outlet for her journalistic ambitions, and a platform for her theories.

LANA LANG

As a child, Lana Lang was famous as the little orphan in the fairy princess costume whose picture on the front cover of *TIME Magazine* was a haunting reminder of the 1989 meteor shower. After her parents' death, she was adopted by her aunt, Nell Potter, and lived with her until Nell married and moved to Metropolis. Although Lana has suffered more than her fair share of heartache during her young life, she is a spirited young woman who charms almost everyone she meets.

FREAK MAGNET

Lana Lang's beauty has caught the interest of some of Smallville's weirdest residents. "Bug boy" Greg Arkin, Adam Knight, Seth Nelson, Tina Greer, and Jason Teague are five of the more disturbed individuals who have been enthralled by Lana.

LANA FACTS

• After successfully redesigning the Talon coffee shop, Lana decided to spend a summer in Paris studying art.

• Lana lived next door to the Kents with her aunt, Nell Potter, until Nell moved to Metropolis to start a new life with her husband.

• After this Lana moved in with Chloe Sullivan and her father, Gabe, so she could stay at Smallville High School with her friends.

FAMILY TRAGEDY

Young Lana watched from across the street as her parents were crushed and instantly killed by a falling meteor rock. The moving image of 3-year-old Ms. Lang was later used on the cover of *TIME Magazine.*

Although fifteen years have passed since the meteor shower, many people in Smallville can never forget that fateful day. Teenager Lana Lang lost both her parents in the shower, and she mourns their loss to this day.

Lewis Lang, 32, and his wife Laura, 30, were on their way to collect their daughter from her aunt when tragedy struck.

"Those memories will live with me forever."

A closer look at Ms. Lang reveals a distinctive green necklace round her neck. It turns out that this is a fragment of meteor rock and serves as a reminder of her parents.

COUNTRY GIRL

Lana loves horses and has won several horseback riding awards. After Lana's aunt Nell moved to Metropolis, Lana stabled her horse Donatello at the Kent farm. Clark Kent was particularly delighted by her frequent visits!

FIRST LOVE

Lana's first serious relationship was with Smallville High's star quarterback, Whitney Fordman. Whitney left Smallville after Lana's freshman year to join the Marines. He later died a hero, a victim of a land mine.

To Lana, Clark Kent was simply the boy next door who acted strangely whenever she was around. However, when she got to know Clark, she began to develop feelings for him, although she often felt that he was keeping something from her.

As a cheerleader and girlfriend of the star quarterback, Lana was very popular in high school. She was the kind of girl that guys wanted to date and other girls wanted to be.

HIDDEN DEPTHS

Lana is a sweet and kind young woman, but sometimes her bad side comes out to play. Seth Nelson's magnetic appeal landed her in jail, while the Nicodemus flower made her indulge in a bit of skinny dipping!

Lana has had to learn how to take care of herself. When the Kents were held hostage by Morgan Edge's associates, she hit one of the gang over the head with a shovel!

HENRY SMALL

When Lana found an old picture of her mother with a man who was not Lewis Lang, she was shocked. She discovered that the man was Henry Small and that he, not Lewis, was her biological father. Lana tried to establish a relationship with her father, but it upset his family, so she backed away.

THE RESCUE

A man like Lex Luthor does not believe in wasting time by observing the speed limit. He loves driving his Porsche at great speeds, and the roads around Smallville are mostly free of traffic.

In many ways, Clark Kent wasn't like other teenagers, thanks to his extraordinary powers and extraterrestrial origins. But in other ways, Clark was just like any other guy his age—he dreamed of being on the football team and dating the prettiest girl in school. When Clark stopped for a while on Loeb Bridge, he just needed some time out to think. However, his peaceful contemplation was interrupted when Lex Luthor's Porsche spun out of control, hitting Clark, and sending them both into the water below.

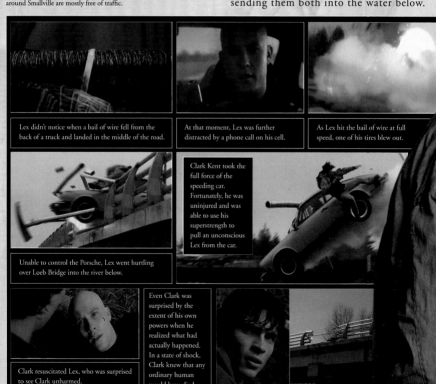

Lex didn't notice when a bail of wire fell from the back of a truck and landed in the middle of the road.

At that moment, Lex was further distracted by a phone call on his cell.

As Lex hit the bail of wire at full speed, one of his tires blew out.

Clark Kent took the full force of the speeding car. Fortunately, he was uninjured and was able to use his superstrength to pull an unconscious Lex from the car.

Unable to control the Porsche, Lex went hurtling over Loeb Bridge into the river below.

Clark resuscitated Lex, who was surprised to see Clark unharmed.

Even Clark was surprised by the extent of his own powers when he realized what had actually happened. In a state of shock, Clark knew that any ordinary human would have died.

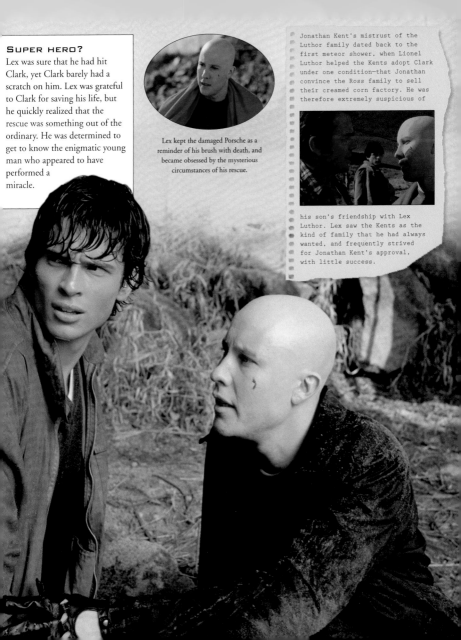

SUPER HERO?

Lex was sure that he had hit Clark, yet Clark barely had a scratch on him. Lex was grateful to Clark for saving his life, but he quickly realized that the rescue was something out of the ordinary. He was determined to get to know the enigmatic young man who appeared to have performed a miracle.

Lex kept the damaged Porsche as a reminder of his brush with death, and became obsessed by the mysterious circumstances of his rescue.

Jonathan Kent's mistrust of the Luthor family dated back to the first meteor shower, when Lionel Luthor helped the Kents adopt Clark under one condition—that Jonathan convince the Ross family to sell their creamed corn factory. He was therefore extremely suspicious of his son's friendship with Lex Luthor. Lex saw the Kents as the kind of family that he had always wanted, and frequently strived for Jonathan Kent's approval, with little success.

LEX LUTHOR

It was never going to be easy growing up as the son of Lionel Luthor, one of the most ruthless and powerful men in Metropolis, but for Alexander "Lex" Luthor, life has always been tough. When he was nine years old, he suffered the permanent loss of his hair in the meteor shower that hit Smallville. He is also haunted by the deaths of his younger brother and his mother when he was twelve years old. Lex's relationship with his father is complex, and it was Lionel who sent him to Smallville, to run LuthorCorp's Fertilizer Plant No. 3.

PLAYBOY BILLIONAIRE

Thanks to his father's fortune, Lex is able to live a privileged lifestyle. He wears the finest clothes, drives the best cars, and flies around the world in a private jet—almost nothing and no one are beyond the reach of the Luthor billions. However, Lex has come to realize the truth of the saying that money cannot buy happiness.

Lex is determined to carve his own identity and emerge from the shadow of his father. In Smallville, Lex's friendship with Clark Kent showed him that people can be good and families can be loving. However, at times Lex cannot help feeling that he has inherited more from his father than just wealth.

UNLUCKY IN LOVE

Lex has always found himself attracted to dark-haired, beautiful women, and has had numerous girlfriends and affairs. Lionel has often speculated that Lex is drawn to women who remind him of his mother. Lex even got married to Dr. Helen Bryce, who betrayed him and left him for dead.

On his honeymoon, Lex survived a plane crash. He was left stranded on a desert island and very nearly went insane!

LUTHOR'S LUCKY ESCAPE!

Further to our reports on the devastation of last week's meteor shower, we bring readers a special report on one of the lucky survivors.

Nine-year-old Alexander "Lex" Luthor was visiting town with his father, Metropolis billionaire owner of LuthorCorp, Lionel Luthor, when the meteors hit. Luthor Snr. was in town to negotiate a deal to buy the old Ross creamed corn factory. A deal that we can exclusively reveal has now been signed.

As the meteor shower began, young Lex found himself alone in a corn field. Running for his life, the frightened young boy

suffered a severe asthma attack, and the next thing he remembers is being found in the flattened corn field by his father, shivering and bizarrely, completely bald.

With the help of local farmer, Jonathan Kent, Luthor rushed his son to the Smallville Medical Center, where he was pronounced lucky to be alive. It is not known at this time if the hair loss is permanent.

Lex's inquiring mind is an asset to him in business. But in his personal life, it often causes him to overstep the boundaries of friendship, especially with Clark.

SHREWD BUSINESSMAN

Lex turned exile in Smallville into a success. He invested wisely, choosing companies and individuals that not only make him money, but also help him with his long term ambitions. When Lionel was in prison, Lex seized the opportunity and skilfully guided LuthorCorp toward record profits.

As a mentor as well as a friend, Lex took Clark to museums and special openings, and gave him advice about dealing with the opposite sex, especially Lana.

LIONEL LUTHOR

LuthorCorp Plaza, Est. 1990 in Metropolis, Kansas

L ionel Luthor tells people that he is from a wealthy family, but in reality he grew up on the seedy streets of Metropolis' Suicide Slum. After graduating from college, Lionel quickly rose to the top of the Metropolis business community, eventually becoming one of the richest men in the world. His company, LuthorCorp, has holdings in more than a dozen countries, and Lionel's influence stretches far and wide.

POWER TRIP

Lionel Luthor's business tactics include lying, cheating, and stealing. He owes his success to the fact that he is so clever he rarely gets caught. Even after a short spell in prison, Lionel came out more powerful than ever.

LuthorCorp's primary interests are pesticides and real estate. However, there are persistent rumors of top secret projects and highly dangerous experiments.

When Lionel Luthor had the Kent farm illegally raided and searched, Jonathan Kent confronted him in the Kawatche caves and the two men fought. The fight sent the glowing octagonal disc flying toward the wall. This would not be the last showdown between Jonathan and Lionel.

LIONEL LUTHOR FACTS

• It has been suggested that Lionel keeps his trademark long mane of hair to mock his bald son.

• Lionel's father, Lachlan, was a petty criminal who once robbed Lana Lang's great-aunt, Louise McCallum.

• Although his wife was a brunette, Lionel likes redheads, such as Martha Kent, Rachel Dunleavy, and Genevieve Teague.

If anyone can penetrate Lionel's tough exterior, it is Martha Kent. Martha caught Lionel's attention from the first time he laid eyes on her in Metropolis. Years later, when he was temporarily blinded, Lionel hired Martha as his assistant. Although Martha was married and very much in love with her husband, Lionel still desired her. When Jonathan passed away, Lionel took the opportunity to make his move.

When Lex gave consent for life-saving surgery, it left Lionel blind and furious.

BODY SWAP

When one of the elements caused an imprisoned Lionel to switch bodies with Clark Kent, Lionel admired his new physique, and discovered that Clark had powers and abilities beyond his wildest dreams! When Lionel returned to his own body, he was completely cured of his terminal liver disease and decided to start a charitable foundation. Fortunately, he had no recollection of his experiences in Clark's body.

JAILED!

Lex Luthor helped the FBI to finally jail his father for the murder of his parents. But even behind bars Lionel remained a threat, and he hired people on the outside to poison his son and drive him insane, although though he later denied that charge.

THE LUTHORS

The Luthor family coat of arms

It seems that the more Lex tries to escape his father's shadow, the more like him he becomes. Lionel's parenting technique is a far cry from the love and warmth that Lex remembers from his late mother. Lionel uses the same tough strategies on his son that have made him such a successful businessman. Ultimately, Lionel has succeeded in what he set out to do—he has created a son as ruthless and as cunning as himself. While this is not the type of man that Lex set out to be, it is the man he has become.

DYSFUNCTIONAL FAMILY

Lillian Luthor suffered postpartum depression after the birth of her second son, Julian. When Lex found the baby no longer breathing, he knew that his mother was responsible. However, when Lionel found him next to the crib, Lex took the blame to spare his mother. Lex only remembered what really happened years later when he was at the Summerholt Institute.

When Lex Luthor discovered the existence of a secret half-brother named Lucas, he brought him to Smallville with hopes of forming a relationship. Lucas is the product of Lionel's affair with Rachel Dunleavy.

LUTHOR FAMILY FACTS

• Though Lionel's personal fortune and his stake in LuthorCorp were reduced to near nothing during his time in prison, he used money stashed in secret off-shore bank accounts to buy his way back into the company.

• When Lionel and Lex are forced to work together, they keep each other at arm's length because they can't trust each other. Lionel taught Lex to keep his friends close and his enemies closer. Lex always heeds this advice.

IN THE ASYLUM

When Lex was about reveal the truth about what Lionel did to his parents, Lionel conspired to poison Lex and make others believe that these claims were insane delusions.

Lionel had Lex committed to the Belle Reve mental institution, where significant portions of Lex's memory were taken away as the result of questionable medical experiments.

REVENGE

After Lex was released from Belle Reve, he got his revenge by working with the FBI to uncover his father's many crimes. When Lionel was put into prison, the tables were suddenly turned and Lionel had to watch his son take control of LuthorCorp.

Despite their strained relationship, both Lionel and Lex are on LuthorCorp's Board of Directors, and they both maintain part-time residence in the Luthor mansion in Smallville. The destiny and interests of father and son seem inextricably linked.

THE LUTHOR MANSION

Lex and Lionel's palatial estate, said to have been imported stone by stone from the Luthor family home in Scotland, is nestled in a secluded, wooded area on the outskirts of Smallville. The mansion's unique design makes it Lowell County's only castle, and it boasts more than 37 rooms, a helicopter pad, a solarium, a library full of rare volumes, servants quarters, and exquisite gardens. The Luthor family estate is the primary dwelling of LuthorCorp CEO Lex Luthor, who spends his time commuting between Smallville and LuthorCorp Plaza in Metropolis.

The Luthors have played host to famous visitors, including royalty, political dignitaries, the wealthiest families in Metropolis and abroad, and even visitors from Hollywood, all curious to see if the legends of ghosts and dungeons are true.

THE MANSION

The property is constructed primarily of sandstone. The main building is 200 feet (61 meters) long and 86 feet (26 meters) wide with an 82 feet (25 meters) high turret. Inside, the rooms are oak and rosewood paneled with teak floors. Priceless art hangs on the walls and the rooms are decorated with rare sculptures and other valuable pieces. The mansion is maintained by a small but loyal staff.

THE LUTHORS MOVE IN

Lex was the first Luthor to settle into the home, and his arrival came months before his father had even been to see it. Clark Kent was one of the first visitors to the mansion, interrupting Lex's fencing practice. Lex was surprised that Clark managed to get past the security gates.

Clark wondered why Lionel would go to all the trouble of moving such a big home from Scotland brick by brick. "Because he can," Lex told him.

LUTHOR GARDENS

The Luthor estate boasts fantastic gardens maintained by two expert gardeners. The gardens feature plants and trees native to the area, as well as some more exotic imported flora and fauna. The grounds also feature several paths and trails which are perfect for gentle strolls or more active jogging routes. It was in these gardens that the body of Bridgette Crosby was found.

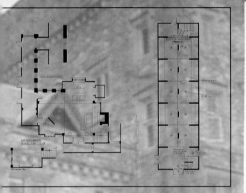

The plans for the Luthor mansion remain faithful to the original building, which is believed to have been constructed in Scotland in about the 13th century, supposedly by Luthor ancestors. The Smallville Luthor mansion does have some modern modifications, such as electricity, running water, and a helicopter pad.

BIZARRE BREAK-IN AT MANSION

Disturbing reports have reached this newspaper concerning an alleged break-in and shooting at the Luthor mansion.

A masked gunman was said to have entered the Luthor mansion this weekend, shooting a security guard. However, when the Smallville sheriff investigated the incident, she could find no evidence of foul play.

Billionaire son of Lionel Luthor, Lex Luthor was also reported to have been injured during the "incident," although sources claim that Luthor's injuries were sustained after jumping through a second-floor window.

Aside from Lex Luthor's injuries there appears to be no evidence of a break-in. Luthor now claims he was set-up by his father and Morgan Edge, a notorious crime boss, who has been missing since October.

Strange goings on indeed at the Luthor mansion, and this newspaper will bring you all the breaking news, as it happens.

MANSION AT NIGHT

The Luthor estate casts a mysterious shadow when viewed at night. A closer look reveals the beautiful fountains illuminated by a myriad of tiny lights. This eerie glow and Gothic aura are unmatched by any other building in rural Smallville.

MANSION SECRETS

Any home belonging to the Luthors is bound to have its secrets. In addition to a labyrinth of hidden tunnels and escape routes, the mansion boasts a high-tech Panic Room and a secret room devoted to Lex's private investigations of Clark Kent. Most rooms in the Luthor mansion are equipped with state-of-the-art security systems, although felons have still been known to find ways into the mansion.

THE LIBRARY

The Luthor library contains more than 20,000 books. Many of them are priceless first editions and rare leather-bound texts which the Luthors have collected over the years. Lex appreciates the books for their value almost as much as for their literary worth.

The mansion is decorated with style in mind rather than comfort.

Multiple screens give Lex access to all areas of the mansion. Thes security cameras are equipped with microphones so Lex can use an intercom system to communicate from the Panic Room.

THE PANIC ROOM

After several situations put himself and his mansion in grave danger, Lex had a state-of-the-art Panic Room installed next to his study. Inside this concealed room Lex could feel secure and monitor everything that was going on inside the mansion.

1. The study
2. Remote-controlled entrance, concealed behind a book shelf
3. A second reinforced-steel bullet and bombproof door
4. Monitors showing every room in the mansion
5. Control panel
6. Supplies, in case of a long confinement in the Panic Room
7. Bed

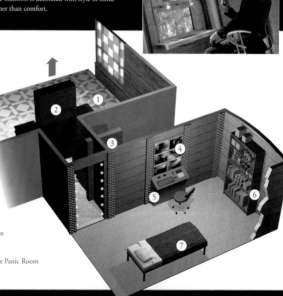

SECRET ROOM

When Clark was given a key by Lionel Luthor, it opened the door to a room devoted to Lex's investigations of a very sensitive topic—Clark Kent. Evidence contained in the room included damaged bullets, incriminating photographs, and a 3-D recreation of the day that Lex ran into Clark on Loeb Bridge.

As well as photographs of the Kent family, Lex's secret room also contained a large chunk of green meteor rock, mixed with some red rocks. Close contact with the rocks made Clark extremely ill.

Lex told Clark that the room was about Lex's own curiosity, and should not affect their friendship.

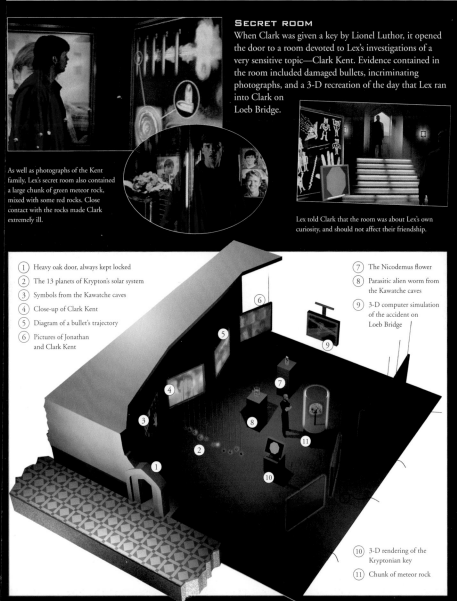

1. Heavy oak door, always kept locked
2. The 13 planets of Krypton's solar system
3. Symbols from the Kawatche caves
4. Close-up of Clark Kent
5. Diagram of a bullet's trajectory
6. Pictures of Jonathan and Clark Kent
7. The Nicodemus flower
8. Parasitic alien worm from the Kawatche caves
9. 3-D computer simulation of the accident on Loeb Bridge
10. 3-D rendering of the Kryptonian key
11. Chunk of meteor rock

WALL OF WEIRD

Chloe Sullivan was one of the first people to realize the connection between the 1989 meteor shower and the strange occurrences in Smallville. As a budding investigative reporter, she gathered evidence and displayed it on her own personal "Wall of Weird." Originally pinned on the *Torch* bulletin board, and later transferred to Chloe's hard drive as a personal database, the Wall of Weird cataloged some of Smallville's strangest citizens and most unexplained phenomena. Chloe believed that mutation for some may have come from exposure at the time of the meteor shower; while for others, powers came from a meteor-based accident.

JODI MELVILLE
Overweight Jodi Melville was sick of being teased by her classmates, so she invented a meteor-based diet shake. The drink made her skinny but left her with an increased hunger to eat the body fat of others.

Jodi was described as a "fat sucking vampire."

MOLLY GRIGGS
Molly made people commit violent acts by sending subliminal messages via cell phones or the internet. She is now part of an underground movement in Metropolis determined to learn the truth about Level 33.1—a secret project of Lex Luthor's that gathers and studies meteor freaks.

TINA GREER
Shapeshifting Tina posed as Le Luthor to rob a bank, killed her mother, and then tried to impersonate Lana Lang. She wa sent to a psychiatric hospital, bu she escaped and later came back to Smallville, pretending to be Whitney Fordman. Tina impale herself during a fight with Clark

ERIC SUMMERS
Eric Summers could absorb the powers of others. When Clark Kent's powers were transferred during a lightning storm, he became violent and irresponsible. As Clark's powers returned, Eric was later transferred to Belle Reve mental asylum.

JUSTIN GAINES
When Justin Gaines was injured in a hit-and-run accident, it activated meteor-induced telekinetic abilities. Justin, a promising young artist who had produced the "Flaming Crow's Feet" cartoons for the *Torch*, came back to Smallville seeking revenge against the careless driver.

SASHA WOODMAN

Sasha Woodman was so desperate to be the class president that she used her freakish ability to control bees to send swarms of them after her opponents. As Sasha's opponents began mysteriously dropping out, Clark entered the class presidential race and soon worked out that Sasha was behind everything.

GREG ARKIN

This bug collector started behaving just like his favorite bugs after a car accident exposed him to meteor rocks. Arkin kidnapped Lana Lang—the object of his long range crush—with the intention of "mating" with her. Fortunately, Clark Kent came to Lana's rescue.

CHRISSY PARKER

Chrissy Parker manages to stay a teenager forever thanks to her unusual power—she has the ability to suck the youth right out of her victims. Although her abilities cannot be linked to the meteor rocks because they pre-date the meteor shower by several decades, this freak still made it onto Chloe's Wall of Weird.

ABBY FINE

Dubbed "Scabby Abby" and teased for her bad skin and mousy appearance, Abby Fine got an amazing new look when her mother, Dr. Elaine Fine, peformed facial surgery using injections of liquid kryptonite. However, when Abby kissed anyone, they imagined that their face was hideously deformed.

IAN RANDALL

ADAM KNIGHT

When Chad Nash died from a rare liver disease, a LuthorCorp experiment involving Clark's blood brought him back to life as "Adam Knight." Adam was an expert computer hacker, martial artist, and a talented pianist. He got close to Lana to learn more about Clark.

Ian Randall was a two-faced kind of guy—when he was wooing Chloe Sullivan, he was also dating Lana Lang at the same time. He killed a teacher while one of his duplicates was spending time with Chloe, creating an alibi. Ian was sent off to the Belle Reve asylum when his split personality came to light.

MORE FREAKS

Bug boys and girls, shape-shifters, fat-sucking vampires, and telekinetic boyfriends aren't the only kind of super-beings created from the meteor rocks. Meteor-enhanced krypto-freaks come in many different forms, and can be very hard to detect if they choose to keep their abilities under control and try to live a normal life. Sadly, many of the meteor freaks in Smallville are unable to resist using their powers for personal gain. In fact, it has been theorized that exposure to the meteors magnifies characteristics, desires, or interests that the individuals already possess, to a dangerous level. However, this theory is purely speculation and has never been scientifically confirmed.

JORDAN CROSS

Just by touching someone, Jordan Cross would foresee their death. However, his vision of cross country Coach Altman's death was unfulfilled when Clark rescued the coach from an oncoming car. Bafflingly, Jordan's vision for Clark showed nothing but a flowing red cape.

SEAN KELVIN

This popular ladies' man took a cold dip in Crater Lake and came out too cool for his own good. In order to to stop himself from freezing to death, Sean Kelvin had to take the body heat from others, killing them in the process. Only Clark Kent's quick thinking prevented Chloe from becoming one of his victims.

HARRY VOLK

As he approached old age, convicted murderer Harry Volk was moved to a convalescent center in Smallville. When he fell into a meteor-rock infested koi pond, octogenarian Harry transformed into a teenager. After escaping, he tried to get revenge against the descendants of the jurors who put him into prison.

ALICIA BAKER

This teleporter had a special relationship with Clark Kent, especially when they learned each other's secrets. Unfortunately, Alicia's behavior was unstable, and when she attacked Lana Lang she was placed in Belle Reve. When she was cured Alicia went back to Smallville, but her return ended in tragedy, thanks to Tim Westcott.

JEREMY CREEK

Jeremy Creek was tied up as the Scarecrow when the first meteor shower hit in 1989. He developed the ability to control electrical currents and was hidden away for twelve years. When he resurfaced, he wanted revenge against the Smallville jocks who had tied him up.

SETH NELSON

A head injury from a snow globe containing kryptonite combined with an MRI scan gave Seth magnetic powers that could control both objects and people. He used his power to make Lana fall in love with him, rob the Talon, and run away with him. Only Clark Kent could stop Seth Nelson.

NATHAN DEAN

Petty criminal Nathan Dean assisted Walt Masterson with a series of armed robberies, but the final attempt landed Masterson in jail. Dean possessed a powerful sonic scream that could shatter glass. It also temporarily blinded Clark Kent, and caused him to develop his superhearing.

"KARA"

Claiming to be from Clark's home planet Krypton, Kara had all of the abilities Clark possessed and more. In reality, she was a vessel created by Jor-El using the body of a missing girl named Lindsay Harrison, with the intention of delivering Clark back to his father in the caves.

KYLA WILLOWBROOK

Kyla of the Kawatche tribe was a "skinwalker" with the ability to transform into a wolf. She was heavily opposed to LuthorCorp's intention of building on the Kawatche lands and bonded with Clark, whom she believed to be Naman of the Kawatche prophesies.

ERIC MARSH

Smallville High baseball jock Eric Marsh and his friends discovered a neat way of obtaining superstrength. They stole inhalers containing melted, refined kryptonite from Lionel Luthor, and tried to kill Clark Kent by throwing him in an incinerator. Of course, Clark managed to escape and Eric and his friends were later arrested.

PERRY WHITE

Perry White used to be one of the most respected reporters in Metropolis. Earning the nickname "Pitbull" for his incisive investigative work, he received several Kerth and Pulitzer Prize nominations. However, his career took a nosedive when, thanks to interference from Lionel Luthor, his employers accused him of "serious errors in judgement." Perry White was reduced to working on a low-budget and lowbrow cable show about the paranormal. This once promising reporter has since become a hard drinker with little passion for his work.

Perry White came to Smallville with the intention of covering the weird meteor phenomena for his *X-Styles* cable television show.

Perry White approached Lex with the offer of information about his father in exchange for everything that Lex knows about Clark Kent.

Chloe Sullivan was surprised to meet one of her journalistic heroes in Smallville!

Perry saw Clark Kent perform amazing feats, including superspeeding to catch a flying tractor. Fortunately, everyone dismissed Perry's claims as the ramblings of a confused alcoholic.

Perry White believed he had discovered Clark's secret. Using Lana as bait, Perry lured Clark to Shoulder Gorge and planned to film him using his powers. Perry dived into the gorge.

Clark instinctively jumped after him, but solar flares had rendered him powerless. Clark and Perry were eventually rescued by Lana and Pete. The whole incident convinced Perry White that Clark Kent's "powers" were a figment of his drunken imagination after all.

SPOTLIGHT ON SMALLVILLE

Perry White and his *X-Styles* team made an unwelcome visit to Smallville this week, looking to reopen old wounds. The paranormal series, now in its third season, takes a look at supernatural phenomena across the United States, and the crew are here to film an episode on the Smallville meteor shower.

White was allegedly ejected from the Wild Coyote bar in Granville for offending some of the clientele. Later in the same day, White was arrested for drunk driving after crashing his car near the Smallville welcome sign. Witnesses claim that White was also seen harrassing Lana Lang,

the manager of the Talon, whose parents were killed in the 1989 meteor shower.

After less than a week, White mysteriously left town without his *X-Styles* piece. White's employers refuse to return our calls, but rumors are rife that White tendered his resignation after his visit to Smallville, and that *X-Styles* is in search of a new host.

MIKHAIL MXYZPTLK

Mikhail used his powers to coax Chloe into a kiss.

E uropean Mikhail Mxzyptlk came to Smallville High as part of the LuthorCorp foreign exchange scholarship arranged by Lionel Luthor. Like many of his ancestors, Mikhail has extraordinarily good luck. Within weeks of arriving in Smallville, he set himself up as a bookmaker for students looking to place bets on the Smallville Crows. Mikhail's power meant that he could control the outcomes of the games and make a fortune from the foolish gamblers.

By saying "fumble" or "trip," Mikhail influenced the game.

Mxyzptlk's meddling caused Clark Kent to lose control of his body and resulted in the serious injury of an opposing player.

When Chloe Sullivan discovered Mikhail's weakness, she transmitted a high-pitched jamming frequency over the stadium's intercom system.

The noise rendered Mikhail powerless.

Eventually Mikhail located Chloe. In the middle of the game, Clark Kent used his superspeed to rescue her and knock Mikhail unconscious.

Lex Luthor found it curious that his father would take an interest in such an average student. But when he saw a demonstration of Mikhail's power he understood, and took him to the top-secret Level 33.1. Although Mikhail's powers seemed to have gone, they eventually returned. Mxzyptlk escaped at his first opportunity and his current location is unknown.

BART "THE FLASH" ALLEN

Clark Kent thought he could move fast, but then he met Bart Allen. Bart's life changed forever when he was struck by a flash of lightning and became the fastest boy alive. Rejected by his parents, Bart had to survive on the streets and soon fell into a life of crime in order to get by. Bart's energetic personality and unwillingness to trust anyone mean that he has never settled in one place for too long. Although he is younger than Clark Kent, Bart is much more confident in his powers, and chooses to exploit them rather than hide them.

t seems that Clark might finally have met his match in Bart—at last he had a race on his hands, one that he could actually lose!

BART ALLEN FACTS

• Bart carries around several fake identification cards, including the names Jay Garrick, Barry Allen, and Wally West.

• Bart's favorite colors are red and yellow, and when he runs fast he is trailed by a red streak.

• When Bart met Chloe Sullivan in the Talon, he threw her the flirtatious line that he was from the future. However, the lack of present-day birth records for Bart Allen indicates that his story may not have been far from the truth.

• Bart thought that gifts would impress his friends, even if they were stolen items.

A drunk driver from Construx Industries fell asleep at the wheel and plowed into a newsstand.

Bart Allen saw the oncoming vehicle, and quick as a flash pulled Jonathan Kent to safety, swiping his wallet in the process.

Bart sold most of the stolen goods to Hanison, a small-time criminal in Suicide Slum.

Clark was able to locate Bart by tracking his Dad's credit card. and went back to Metropolis to confront him.

Clark pursued Bart in a high-speed chase, but Bart ran over a body of water and got away.

Frustrated that he had been unable to catch Bart, Clark returned home to Smallville, where he was greeted by an unexpected house guest.

When Bart discovered that Lex Luthor possessed a valuable piece of artwork he used his speed to bypass security and steal it. He then tried to sell it to Hanison.

LADIES' MAN

Bart is a fast talker as well as a fast mover, especially with the opposite sex. His cocky, flirtatious attitude had him coming on pretty strongly with Chloe, who found herself rather charmed by him.

Hanison tried to double cross Bart and sell the artwork back to Lex Luthor. When Hanison's plan failed, he pulled a gun on Bart, threatening to test if he was "faster than a speeding bullet."

Fortunately, Clark arrived at superspeed and stopped Hanison from shooting Bart.

SPEED FREAKS

Bart criticized Clark for seeing his powers as a curse. He challenged him to have some fun, so the "two super-powered young studs" took a quick trip to Miami. Clark was sad to say goodbye to Bart.

Clark sent Hanison flying out of his garage and into a trailer next door!

Bart told Clark that he might consider staying in Smallville if Clark could catch him. This is one race that Clark will never win!

HIGH SCHOOL YEARBOOK

Established in the late 19th century, Smallville High School is one of Kansas' oldest higher learning establishments and has more than 1300 students. Current principal Terrance Reynolds encourages his students to achieve the highest possible amount of greatness. A transfer from the illustrious Excelsior Prep in Metropolis with degrees from both Harvard and Columbia, he demands punctuality and respect, and challenges his students to plan properly for their futures.

PRINCIPAL REYNOLDS

THE CROWS

For years, Smallville High had a winning football team coached by the late Walt Arnold. Important alumni from the team include Jonathan Kent, Ethan Miller, Whitney Fordman, and Clark Kent. The current team is coached by Wayne Quigley, a former Crows quarterback.

Though Chloe's body was present to accept her Prom crown, it was actually possessed by classmate Dawn Stiles.

PROM QUEEN

Chloe Sullivan posted an editorial in the *Torch* saying that "the election of Prom royalty is an archaic and elitist ritual whose time has come and gone," which made the Prom nothing more than a "popularity contest." To her surprise, however, the editorial got her nominated and later chosen by her peers as Smallville High's Prom Queen.

Everyone at the Prom was shocked at the acceptance speech given by "Chloe," who told everyone that Dawn Stiles was more deserving of the honor.

Most likely to...

Have a happy marriage
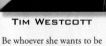

MANDY WALSH

Be drafted to the NFL

CLARK KENT

Marry a billionaire

LANA LANG

Have plastic surgery

DAWN STILES

Become mayor of Smallville

TIM WESTCOTT

Win the Pulitzer Prize

CHLOE SULLIVAN

Win a Nobel Prize

WENDELL JOHNSON

Travel the world

ALICIA BAKER

Be whoever she wants to be

TINA GREER

Be liked, wherever he goes

PETE ROSS

Live for a hundred years

CHRISSY PARKER

Stay in Smallville forever

BRENDAN NASH 47

KAWATCHE CAVES

The underground caves held sacred by the Kawatche tribe offered Clark Kent the first clues to his true origins. Visitors with ties to Krypton, including Clark's own father Jor-El, have connections to the caves' hidden areas and the hieroglyphics that cover the walls. The caves became a point of curiosity not just for Clark Kent, but also for Lex and Lionel Luthor, who fought over custodianship of the caves, desperate to unlock the secrets contained within them.

DAGGER OF NAMAN

This ancient blade gave promising student Jeremiah Holdsclaw amazing abilities. It also led him to believe that he was Naman and that Lionel Luthor was Segeth. However, when Lionel and Lex Luthor simultaneously reached to grab the blade it disintegrated. Segeth was revealed, but which Luthor was he?

When Clark lost his memory for a short time, Lex took advantage of the situation. He obtained a map Clark had done of the caves and tried to find out more of their secrets.

Kyla found Clark after he fell into the caves. She was Professor Willowbrook's granddaughter and had inherited his skinwalker abilities. She was able to transform into a wolf.

ANCIENT ART DISCOVERED

Caves containing paintings said to be over 500 years old have been discovered in Smallville. The caves, located on land earmarked for the proposed LuthorCorp Corporate Plaza, were discovered by Clark Kent. Clark, the son of local farmers Jonathan and Martha Kent, found the caves following a motorbike accident in which he was thrown from the vehicle and fell into the caves.

The cave artwork appears to be Kawatche in origin. Professor Joseph Willowbrook of the University of Kansas Center for Indigenous Nations Studies,

himself a Kawatche, has petitioned the Lowell County Council to protect what he believes is sacred land.

Today it has emerged that LexCorp, run by Lex Luthor, has secured the contract for the custodianship of the caves, and Mr. Luthor promises that plans to build on the site have been postponed indefinitely.

THE PROPHECY OF NAMAN

Kyla Willowbrook told Clark her tribe's legend of Naman, a man who fell from the skies in a rain of fire, who would have superstrength and shoot fire from his eyes.

The visitor from the stars supposedly brought special green stones that had strange effects on people, and it was at this time that the first skinwalkers appeared. The cave walls also displayed Kryptonian symbols.

Naman had an arch-rival named Segeth, whom the prophecies said would be his deadliest foe in a never-ending battle. Several of the paintings represented the struggle between Naman and Segeth.

ALIEN PARASITES

Creatures lying dormant in the cave walls were awakened during a student party. They punctured victims in the back of the neck, enlarging their adrenal glands. Victims began to act impulsively to feel the ultimate adrenaline rush. Pete and Chloe were both infected, and some students died. Dr. Walden's tests concluded that they were alien parasites.

KRYPTONIAN DOWNLOAD

By placing the octagonal key in a similarly-shaped hole in the Kawatche caves, Clark was downloaded with information about his origins. He also acquired the ability to understand the Kryptonian language, which a short time later enabled him to decipher the message from Dr. Swann.

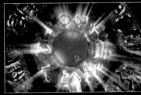

The information flowed through Clark like a supercharged download.

UNLOCKING THE SECRETS

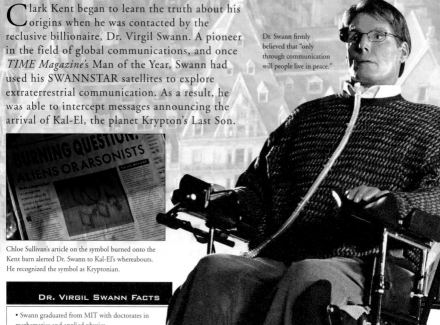

Clark Kent began to learn the truth about his origins when he was contacted by the reclusive billionaire, Dr. Virgil Swann. A pioneer in the field of global communications, and once *TIME Magazine*'s Man of the Year, Swann had used his SWANNSTAR satellites to explore extraterrestrial communication. As a result, he was able to intercept messages announcing the arrival of Kal-El, the planet Krypton's Last Son.

Dr. Swann firmly believed that "only through communication will people live in peace."

Chloe Sullivan's article on the symbol burned onto the Kent barn alerted Dr. Swann to Kal-El's whereabouts. He recognized the symbol as Kryptonian.

DR. VIRGIL SWANN FACTS

• Swann graduated from MIT with doctorates in mathematics and applied physics.

• At one time, Swann Communications had over 45 satellites in orbit around the planet Earth.

• Swann donated a major portion of his company's profits toward the US space program, and in return was given unprecedented access to extraterrestrial findings.

MEETING DR. SWANN

Dr. Swann contacted Clark via email, using the Kryptonian symbol of "hope" to show that he was genuine. He showed Clark messages from the day of the first meteor shower. The first message said "This is Kal-El of Krypton. Our infant son, our last hope. Please protect him and deliver him from evil."

A second Kryptonian message said that Kal-El's parents, Jor-El and Lara, would be with him, "for all the days of your life."

Dr. Steven Hamilton wrote a controversial paper on the effects of the meteor rocks. He was widely discredited, lost his job at Metropolis University, and was reduced to selling novelty meteor rocks on a Smallville roadside. He was later employed by Lex Luthor, but extended exposure to the meteor rocks caused Hamilton to suffer "jitters." He was eventually killed when doused by green liquid from the meteor rocks.

Walden was blasted with a beam of light when he tried to put Clark's octagonal disc into the cave wall.

Kryptonian symbols were burned into the ceiling of Walden's padded room at the Smallville Medical Center.

DR. WALDEN

Dr. Frederick Walden was a cryptologist recruited by Lex Luthor to decipher the symbols in the Kawatche caves. When an accident left Walden in a catatonic state, his brain began functioning at a heightened rate. He eventually awoke and began babbling that "the day is coming."

Walden accidentally burned to death, but the imprint of the octagonal disc was left on his hand.

SPACESHIP

The Kents discovered a rectangular key inside Clark's spaceship on the day they found him. After Clark learned how to decipher the Kryptonian language, he realized it was his ship's heart. As his father Jonathan looked on, Clark inserted it into the ship to hear Jor-El's final message.

The third message from Krypton said "On this third planet from this star Sol, you will be a god among men. They are a flawed race. Rule them with strength, my son. That is where your greatness lies."

This message was from Jor-El to Jonathan Kent, and it informed him that he was waiting for Clark to be delivered to him.

PREMATURE GOODBYE

During their second meeting, Dr. Swann showed Clark a new message that seemed to be intended for someone else. Sadly, this proved to be Clark's last meeting with Dr. Swann. Just before he died, Swann returned the octagonal disc to Clark and gave him some final advice to follow his destiny.

CLARK'S ORIGINS

B ecause he was so young when he was sent
to Earth, Clark has no memory of his
parents or his native planet. From the messages
deciphered by Dr. Swann and conversations
with Jor-El, he has learned that he is Krypton's
Last Son, sent to Earth before his planet was
destroyed. Messages from Jor-El suggest that
he was sent to Earth to conquer it. However,
Clark can't help feeling that his place on Earth
is to help people.

Kal-El's ship was made from
high-density materials,
designed to withstand
a journey of billions of
miles. It was built by
Jor-El—one of Krypton's
greatest scientists.

DOOMED PLANET

Jor-El and Lara sent Kal-El to Earth to save him from
Krypton's destruction. As Lara placed her infant son
into the spaceship, she was worried that he would not
be loved or cared for in his new home, demonstrating
a compassion that is rare in Kryptonians.

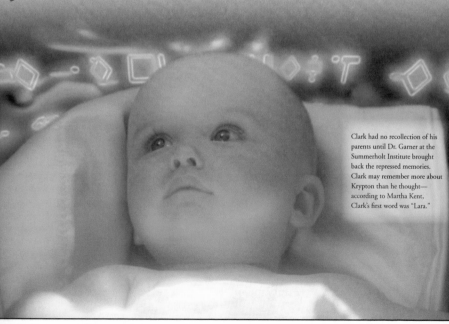

Clark had no recollection of his
parents until Dr. Garner at the
Summerholt Institute brought
back the repressed memories.
Clark may remember more about
Krypton than he thought—
according to Martha Kent,
Clark's first word was "Lara."

While Lara may have been concerned about who would take care of her son, it appears that Jor-El was more certain of Kal-El's destiny. Could his own connection to Smallville have influenced him when plotting the spaceship's course? Combined with the Kryptonian lettering and the symbols in the Kawatche caves, Krypton has a deep connection to Smallville, which has not yet been fully explored.

DISCIPLES OF ZOD

Aethyr and Nam-Ek are two Kryptonian warriors who arrived with the second meteor shower. They are disciples of Jor-El's nemesis, General Zod, and the first true Kryptonians Clark Kent ever faced. They are currently in the Phantom Zone, an eternal prison to which Clark will later be sent.

MISSING PLANET

When Dr. Swann tried to find the source of the signal announcing Kal-El's arrival, he discovered that Krypton no longer existed. Later, Professor Fine lied to Clark that Jor-El was a violent dictator who caused Krypton's destruction and killed billions. In reality, Brainiac just wanted Clark to help him free Zod. The truth of how and why Krypton was destroyed is unknown.

ARRIVAL

Baby Kal-El's journey took the equivalent of three Earth years. He arrived in Smallville in a shower of meteors, the last remnants of his home planet Krypton. Kal-El exited the ship and greeted his new parents—the Kents.

PLANET KRYPTON FACTS

• Although Lara displayed compassion, Kryptonians were cold and unfeeling by nature. Most Kryptonian births were the result of test-tube gestation matrices.

• Although Jor-El told the people of Krypton that their planet was about to explode, his warnings were ignored.

• Krypton orbited a red sun by the name of Rao. Rao was worshipped as patron deity by the people of the planet.

KRYPTONITE

The meteor shower that devastated Smallville in 1989 was actually the last remnants of Clark's home planet, Krypton, which had exploded. What the Smallville folk call "meteor rocks" is in fact kryptonite. Different variations of kryptonite have been discovered since the meteor shower and have different effects on both Kryptonians and humans. These rocks give humans powers beyond their wildest imagination, but for Clark Kent, these little pieces of home have potentially deadly effects.

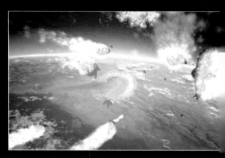

The remaining fragments of the planet Krypton traveled millions of light years to reach their final destination of Smallville, Kansas.

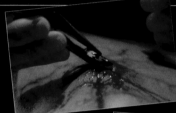

Clark is bulletproof, except when the bullets are green kryptonite. When meteor freak hunter Van McNulty shot him with kryptonite bullets, Clark's parents had to work fast to save him from the deadly poison.

When Clark was dipped into this kryptonite tub for Dr. Garner's memory experiment, even he could not escape.

GREEN KRYPTONITE

This is the most common form of meteor rock and is still found in abundance in many locations in Smallville. In humans, green kryptonite can cause different degrees of reaction, depending on the type of exposure. In some cases it can produce temporary effects such as weight loss or hallucinations, but in the most extreme cases it can cause severe mutation. For Kryptonians like Clark, green kryptonite causes sickness and the loss of his powers.

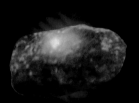

Clark discovered that lead can shield him from the effects of kryptonite. When he put some into a lead-lined box, he felt nothing.

When Lionel Luthor made a copy of the octagonal key in green kryptonite, Clark needed all his strength to cope with his allergic reaction.

RED KRYPTONITE

This form of kyrptonite, also known as Red K, only seems to affect Kryptonians. Its powers were first discovered when the cheap rocks were used to make the Smallville High class rings. The ring made gentle farm boy Clark Kent headstrong, dangerous, reckless, and violent. Red K works like most other addictive drugs—for Clark it brings out his wild side and makes him lose any inhibitions. Clark's friends and family will do anything they can to keep him away from the dangerous red rock.

Teleporter Alicia Baker knew the effect that red kryptonite had on Clark, so she made him a Red K necklace. When Clark wore the necklace he acted on impulse.

Alicia convinced Red K Clark to go to Las Vegas and get married. However, the necklace broke in the honeymoon suite and Clark quickly came to his senses.

BLACK KRYPTONITE

The Swann Foundation first revealed this type of kryptonite when Bridgette Crosby gave it to Martha Kent to turn Kryptonian Kal back into Clark. Black kryptonite occurs when green kryptonite is subjected to intense heat, and its main effect is the separation of a person into two halves—good and bad.

When Martha used the black kryptonite on Kal, he split in two. The good side—Clark—and the bad side—Kal—fought for control before Clark won and the two sides merged together.

Black kryptonite works on humans, too. A LuthorCorp experiment accidentally created black kryptonite and split Lex in two.

SILVER KRYPTONITE

This is not a true kryptonite as it was artificially created by Brainiac. It was sent to Lana Lang's dorm, claiming to be from Lex Luthor, although he denied it. A splinter from the silver rock infected Clark and resulted in serious paranoia and delusions, which made him angry and dangerous.

Clark imagined his worst fears come to life—his parents working with Lionel Luthor, Lana falling in love with Lex, and Chloe revealing his secrets.

Under the influence of silver kryptonite, Clark believed that Lana had feelings for Lex.

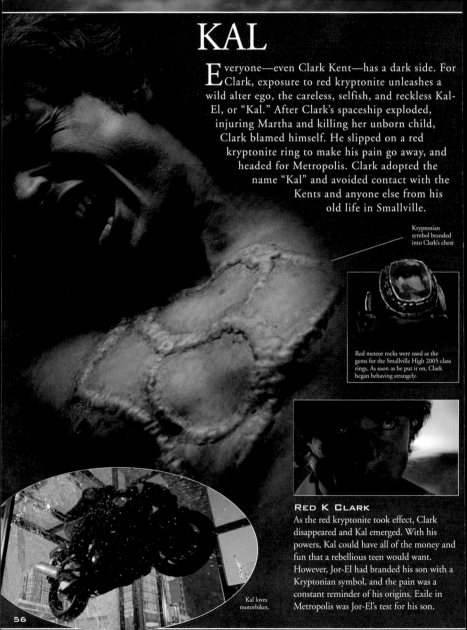

KAL

Everyone—even Clark Kent—has a dark side. For Clark, exposure to red kryptonite unleashes a wild alter ego, the careless, selfish, and reckless Kal-El, or "Kal." After Clark's spaceship exploded, injuring Martha and killing her unborn child, Clark blamed himself. He slipped on a red kryptonite ring to make his pain go away, and headed for Metropolis. Clark adopted the name "Kal" and avoided contact with the Kents and anyone else from his old life in Smallville.

Kryptonian symbol branded into Clark's chest

Red meteor rocks were used as the gems for the Smallville High 2005 class rings. As soon as he put it on, Clark began behaving strangely.

Kal loves motorbikes.

RED K CLARK

As the red kryptonite took effect, Clark disappeared and Kal emerged. With his powers, Kal could have all of the money and fun that a rebellious teen would want. However, Jor-El had branded his son with a Kryptonian symbol, and the pain was a constant reminder of his origins. Exile in Metropolis was Jor-El's test for his son.

CRIME BOSS

Morgan Edge, a childhood friend of Lionel Luthor, and his Intergang have ruled the Metropolis underworld for more than twenty years. When Edge heard about Kal's abilities he knew he could be useful to him and set about tracking him down.

BULLETPROOF BANK ROBBER!

Over $200,000 was stolen yesterday in an audacious raid on the high security Bank of Metropolis. Two police cruisers were severely damaged following the daring heist which, unbelievably, appeared to be carried out by a single masked robber of unusual strength and speed.

Eyewitness reports describe a motorcycle-riding masked man who demonstrated some amazing abilities, which left the police baffled. Some even claim that the man was able to shoot heat from his eyes, which resulted in the damage to the police cruisers. However, the official police statement denies this, saying that the car explosions were due to "an overheating malfunction."

> "We shot 3 rounds into the guy. And he kept going."
>
> Police spokesperson

Police were unable to capture the bank robber despite opening fire at point blank range. The robber remains at large and could strike again at any time.

KEEPING SECRETS

Chloe Sullivan bumped into Clark while out clubbing with friends from the *Daily Planet*. She kept his secret, hoping that Clark would eventually come to his senses.

When Lana finally managed to get the truth out of Chloe, she went to Metropolis to try and persuade Clark to come home. But even she could not get through to bad boy Kal.

OUT OF EXILE

Desperate to have his son back, Jonathan made a deal with Jor-El. Jor-El temporarily gave him powers like Clark's, and Jonathan set off for Metropolis to bring his son home. As father and son fought, the red kryptonite ring was destroyed. The Kryptonian brand disappeared and Clark returned home to resume his normal life.

Jonathan's bargain with Jor-El came at a price—one day he would have to return Clark to Jor-El.

METROPOLIS

Metropolis, the self-styled "city of tomorrow," is the home of some of the country's largest businesses, including LuthorCorp, S.T.A.R. Labs, and the *Daily Planet*. The LuthorCorp Plaza is one of the tallest facilities in Metropolis. It is the head office for the conglomerate run by Lex and Lionel Luthor, and it is said that the building has hidden levels where secret experiments take place.

Although Metropolis is only three hours away from Smallville, it couldn't be more different from the sleepy rural town. Life in Metropolis is fast-paced, and it is certainly not safe to roam the streets alone. The crime-ridden streets of Suicide Slum are a far cry from Smallville's country roads. While his friends Chloe and Lex Luthor hail from Metropolis, country boy Clark Kent wasn't quite sure what to expect on his early visits to the city. Now, with Lana and Chloe attending Metropolis University and Chloe also interning at the *Daily Planet*, Clark splits his time between Smallville and Metropolis. Thankfully for him, his superspeed cuts down the commuting time!

The *Daily Planet* is the most popular newspaper in the United States. It was founded in 1775 by Joshua Merriwether and has been going strong ever since. The Planet prints two daily editions and has a circulation of more than 5 million readers.

THE BIG APRICOT

Metropolis is one of the largest cities in the mid-United States, boasting a population of 3 million at the most recent census. It is home to the all-conquering Metropolis Sharks football team and the Metropolis Meteors baseball team. The city's popular mayor, Frank Berkowitz, has served Metropolis for four successive terms, and a state-of-the-art mass transit system offers Metropolis residents the highest standard of public transportation.

Clark was given the grand tour of Metropolis University by former Smallville High football star Geoff Johns, who had become one of Met U's top players. But like Clark, Geoff was hiding secret abilities.

METROPOLIS UNIVERSITY

Met U offered Clark a football scholarship, but when he learned about Geoff Johns' use of his paralyzing power on the field, he realized that it would be unethical to use his gifts as a free ride toward a scholarship. Now, Met U counts Chloe Sullivan and Lana Lang among its student population.

CITY GIRL

During her high school years, Chloe faked her death, was blackmailed by Lionel Luthor, and finally learned the truth about Clark Kent. Now a college student in Metropolis, Chloe Sullivan has moved on from the inquisitive young girl who printed her meteor theories in the *Torch*. Her high school experiences have increased her commitment to a career in journalism and strengthened her determination to succeed. Chloe remains hopelessly in love with her best friend, Clark Kent.

Lionel Luthor knew that if anyone could provide him with information about Clark Kent, it would be Chloe Sullivan. When Chloe refused, Lionel threatened her father's job.

Chloe has always looked up to her older cousin Lois, but now she recognizes that Lois is in need of direction in her life, and suggests that she tries journalism. Lois isn't too keen at first...

RESOURCEFUL

In addition to her network of contacts, Chloe has learned how to obtain DMV records, hack into Metropolis University's student locator systems, and access the *Daily Planet* news archives. She rarely fails to get the information she needs.

Chloe's troubled mother left the family when her daughter was very young and was later committed to a mental institution. When a LuthorCorp experiment went wrong, it revealed people's deepest and darkest fears. It showed that Chloe was secretly worried that one day she would become mentally ill, just like her mother.

SECRET DISCOVERED

Despite Clark's frequent disappearances and inexplicable behavior, Chloe only learned his secret thanks to Alicia Baker. Alicia fooled Clark into thinking she needed rescuing and when Clark stopped a car with his bare hands, a stunned Chloe was right there to witness it!

After this, Chloe became Clark's closest confidante and the brains behind his brawn.

Editor-in-chief Pauline Kahn, who received a prestigious Kerth Award in the 1980s for a story on the 'Star Wars' missile defense program, wanted to see if Chloe was tough enough to be a reporter.

THE *DAILY PLANET*

The *Torch* was small-town stuff— Chloe is ready to join the big league. She applied for an internship at the *Daily Planet,* but Pauline Kahn refused to give her a job. She later changed her mind and Chloe is now on her way to becoming a reporter.

LOIS LANE

Lois's mother died when she was very young, and as a result Lois and her younger sister Lucy were left in the care of their father, five-star general Sam Lane. Lois' father's job in the U.S. Army meant that the family often moved around, and never had any permanent home. With the general often absent on army business, Lois was also left to care for her younger sister. As a result, Lois grew up faster than most girls her age.

TOUGH COOKIE

Lois Lane, a forthright young woman still in search of her path in life, found herself in Smallville following the supposed death of her cousin, Chloe Sullivan. She was deeply upset by her cousin's death and resolved to uncover all the suspicious circumstances surrounding her demise.

While Lois stayed with the general, Lucy was sent to boarding school in Europe. When she turned up in Smallville, it was all part of a scam to steal money from Lex Luthor. Lucy escaped with one of Lex's cars and the cash, leaving her heartbroken sister behind.

General Sam Lane tries to run his family like the military. This has given Lois her tough exterior, and she always refers to her father as "the General."

STUDENT FOUND ALIVE!

...vents surrounding the tragic death of local high school student Chloe Sullivan took a dramatic turn yesterday as the deceased girl's cousin, Lois Lane, arrived in Smallville in search of answers about what really happened.

Chloe Sullivan had been part of a Witness Protection Program as she waited to testify against Lionel Luthor in his forthcoming trial, so her death immediately seemed suspicious.

Plucky Ms. Lane, daughter of five-star General Sam Lane, lost no time in visiting her cousin's grave. As if guided by X-ray vision, Ms. Lane dug up her

cousin's grave, only to find that it was empty.

Later, with the help of local boy Clark Kent, Ms. Lane discovered her cousin safe and very much alive, although shaken by her near-death ordeal.

Thanks to Lois Lane, Ms. Sullivan is due to take the witness stand against Lionel Luthor next week.

CLOSE COUSINS

Lois and Chloe are good friends as well as cousins. Now that Chloe is based in Metropolis, Lois spends her free time hanging out with Chloe at the *Daily Planet.* She is really starting to like it there...

Though she pretends to dislike him, Lois has a soft spot for Clark and his family. Clark too is more fond of Lois than he will admit.

LOIS AND CLARK

When Lois first met Clark he was naked and suffering from amnesia. In no time at all she had turned him out of his bedroom and taken over his family! Lois has also grown close to Martha Kent, who has become a good friend and mother figure.

LOIS LANE FACTS

- Lois learned that she was missing some of the credits necessary to graduate high school so she enrolled at Smallville High.

- Lois was expelled from Met U after an incident involving underage drinking.

- Lois became one of Jonathan Kent's strongest supporters in the race for senator, even becoming his campaign manager.

- Lois is horribly allergic to Shelby, the Kents' dog.

MOVING ON

In the summer before her senior year at Smallville High, Lana left her friends behind and departed for Paris in search of life beyond the small town she had grown up in. She had always dreamed of leaving Smallville to find excitement and new challenges, and Paris proved to be everything she hoped it would be, and more. Lana loved life in France and spent the summer studying art and trying to forget about Clark Kent. However, something happened to Lana in Paris that brought her back to Smallville for answers.

When Lana touched the tomb of medieval Countess Margaret Isobel Theroux, she was suddenly bathed in light. The next thing she remembered was waking up in her apartment twelve hours later with a mysterious tattoo on her lower back.

NEW LOVE

Lana found love in Paris with Jason Teague, a fellow American touring Europe to escape his wealthy parents. After Clark's secretive behavior, Lana found Jason's honesty very attractive. When Lana abruptly left Paris to return to Smallville, Jason followed her home, and they resumed their relationship. Things were good for a time.

LANA LANG FACTS

- Dating Lana Lang may be a kiss of death—Whitney Fordman, Adam Knight, and Jason Teague all met untimely deaths.
- When Lana moved to Metropolis for college, Lois Lane took over her apartment above the Talon.
- Lana almost became addicted to a deadly kryptonite injection because it allowed her to "see" her parents again.

ana Lang was amazed when
he saw two aliens emerging
rom a spaceship after the
econd meteor shower. Her
uriosity brought her to
ex Luthor, who worked with
er to find out more. This
lien encounter, combined
ith interest in the meteor
hower that killed her
arents, helped inspire
ana to study astronomy at
etropolis University.
owever, in spite of her
tudies, Lana does not
uspect the truth
bout Clark.

COUNTESS THOREAU

Lana's investigation into her strange tattoo led her to the
spellbook of Countess Margaret Isobel Thoreau. As she read
aloud from the book, the Countess's spirit possessed Lana's
body, resulting in wild behavior she could not control.

Isobel's spirit left
Lana as soon as
she killed
Genevieve Teague
with one of the
Kryptonian
elements.

VAMPIRE SORORITY

A late entrant to Met U, Lana
pledged the Tri-Psi sorority so that
she could live on campus. However,
membership of the sorority is for
life—they are immortal vampires.
Clark only saved Lana by plunging
a syringe into her heart.

PAYING THE PRICE

After keeping his secret for so many years,
Clark decided that the time was right to tell
Lana. Tragically, the chain of events from
that moment led to Lana's death. Devastated,
Clark appealed to Jor-El to reset time and
give him a second chance. This time Clark
did not reveal the truth and Lana survived.

THE TEAGUES

Genevieve Teague was so manipulative that Jason wondered if his mother had arranged for him to meet Lana in Paris.

When Lana first met Jason Teague in Paris, he seemed exactly what she was looking for—an honest, romantic young man who was completely open with her at all times. Lana too seemed perfect for Jason—a beautiful and passionate young woman who wasn't simply interested in him for his wealth. However, when Lana returned to Smallville and Jason quickly followed her, their old lives soon caught up with them, and their relationship was put to the test.

Jason's mother appeared in Lana's dream the night before she met Genevieve for the first time. Lana was dreaming of Isobel burning at the stake, while a woman resembling Genevieve Teague watched. Lana was having a vision of her own ancestor and of Genevieve's.

FOOTBALL COACH

In need of money after being cut off by his parents, Jason took a job as assistant coach for the Smallville High Crows. He had to keep his relationship with Lana secret because it was against school rules to date a student.

Clark respected Jason as a coach and valued his advice, until he found out about his relationship with Lana.

JASON AND LANA

When Jason and Lana's relationship became public knowledge, Jason was fired from his job at Smallville High. When Lex Luthor suggested that Jason work for him, Lana was deeply suspicious.

Genevieve Teague was determined to find the elements, and tried to use both Lex and Lionel Luthor to get what she wanted. Father and son were attracted to Mrs. Teague, but she was unable to manipulate them.

ON THE EDGE
A desperate Jason Teague held the Luthors hostage to gain possession of Lionel's element. As the Luthors escaped, Jason was going to shoot Lex until Lionel intervened.

TEAGUE FACTS

• Genevieve's husband, and Jason's father, was wealthy international attorney Edward Teague.

• Jason Teague was a starting quarterback for the Met U Bulldogs before his career was ended by an injury.

• Lex Luthor covered up Genevieve's death to protect Lana. All the evidence suggested that Genevieve and Jason Teague were killed in the second meteor shower.

Genevieve confronted Lana with a gun because she believed that Lana had the missing Water element.

THE ELEMENTS

The quest for three Kryptonian elements interested many people in Smallville. Lex Luthor searched the world for these powerful crystals; Genevieve Teague had her own plan, one that would lead her to cross paths with her son's girlfriend, Lana Lang; and Lionel Luthor also schemed to get a hold of them. Ultimately, however, the elements were intended for Clark Kent, and when combined, they would bring him knowledge beyond his wildest imagination.

Lana found the Kryptonian Water symbol tattooed on her back after tracing an image of the Countess Thoreau.

COUNTESS THOREAU

The soul of Lana's ancestor, the Countess Margaret Isobel Thoreau, took over Lana's body when she was in China searching for the Fire element. She too had a plan for the three elements.

FIRE

Lex Luthor scoured the globe and ended up locating the Fire element within an ancient statue of the Egyptian sun god Ra. Lex quickly left Egypt, ready to take his well-earned prize home to Smallville.

The elements were adorned with Kryptonian symbols like the ones found in the Kawatche caves.

Clark, as the all-Kryptonian, emotionless "Kal," flew halfway across the world, forced his way into Lex Luthor's jet, and stole the Fire element. Lex had no idea who the culprit was.

WATER

Once again possessing Lana's body, Isobel was able to use her spellbook to conjure up the spirits of her best friends, who then possessed the bodies of Lois and Chloe and tried to extract crucial information from Clark.

Isobel donned a ceremonial Chinese outfit when she took possession of Lana's body in Shanghai.

The Water element was located within a statue of a Mayan rain god in Honduras.

AIR

A centuries-old map that Lex Luthor obtained revealed the Air element's true location within a Chinese temple. When Jason and Lex went to China, they were tortured by Chinese authorities.

Because Isobel's powers were magical, she was able to hurt Clark. However, Clark was unwilling to harm Lana, whose body Isobel had possessed.

Lana Lang had possession of the Air element after the journey to China, and hid it from the others.

Lionel Luthor poisoned Genevieve to force her to give him the Water element.

FORTRESS OF SOLITUDE

The merging of the three Kryptonian elements transported Clark thousands of miles away from the Kawatche caves in Smallville to a deserted, icy plain in the Arctic. There he witnessed the formation of the majestic building which would become his Fortress of Solitude. This building, mirroring the architecture of Clark's home planet Krypton, will serve as a place where Clark can learn more about his origins from his Kryptonian father and a place where he doesn't need to hide who he is. In the Fortress of Solitude, Clark can truly be himself.

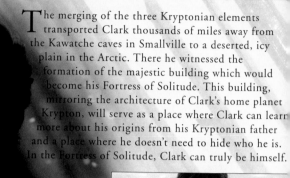

THE ELEMENTS

Clark threw the combined element crystal and it landed on the snowy ground.

The three elements combined to form a single crystal.

To Clark's amazement, a huge structure began to form on the spot, unlike anything he had ever seen before.

When inside the Fortress, Clark can discover more about who he really is by communicating with Jor-El. He also learns important lessons about his Kryptonian heritage.

FORTRESS FACTS

• Placing the octagonal key in a slot inside the Kawatche caves transports Clark to the Fortress of Solitude.

• The Fortress of Solitude covers an area of several square miles, and Clark has yet to discover many of its secrets.

• Some of the crystals in the Fortress have special powers.

• Brainiac tried to fool Clark into poisoning the Fortress in his first bid to free Zod.

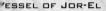

VESSEL OF JOR-EL

After saving Chloe, Clark became mortal and later "died" from a gunshot wound. He found himself transported to the Fortress of Solitude by someone who looked exactly like Lionel Luthor. Jor-El was using Lionel's body as a vessel. He explained to Clark that he could restore his life and return all of his powers, but at a terrible price—the life force of someone close to Clark would be taken in exchange.

Clark had no choice—he could not negotiate with Jor-El, and he had to face his darkest hour knowing that someone he loved was about to die.

When Clark decided to reveal his secret to Lana Lang, he told her to wear warm clothes, then took her to the Fortress of Solitude. There he revealed the truth about himself and asked her to marry him. Lana needed time to think things over, but she eventually said yes. However, after telling Lex the happy news, Lana "died" in a car accident. A heartbroken Clark made the decision to reverse time so that Lana could live, but she has no memory of these events.

Chloe revealed to Clark that she knows his secret and that she didn't need to hide it from her anymore.

TRUE FRIENDSHIP

Chloe nearly died of hypothermia when she was transported to the Fortress. Clark begged Jor-El to spare her life, but in doing so, Jor-El temporarily stripped Clark of his powers and made him an ordinary mortal. Clark would have paid any price to save his best friend.

CLARK & LANA

Clark knew from the first time he saw her that he wanted to get acquainted with Lana Lang. At first shyness and the effects of Lana's necklace meant that he preferred to gaze at her longingly through his telescope. Eventually the two became friends, forming a special bond as they shared their experiences of growing up as orphans. Subsequently, Clark and Lana embarked on a rollercoaster relationship—deeply in love with each other but pulled apart by Clark's secret, which he dare not risk sharing with Lana.

THE TALON

While Lana was managing the Talon, she and Clark would often meet up there to study or just to hang out. This time together helped them grow more comfortable around each other and strengthened their mutual attraction.

When Clark and Lana shared a dance at the Smallville High Prom, one of Clark's most cherished dreams came true.

KEEPING SECRETS

Lana had to put up with broken dates, unexplained situations, and odd requests. She knew that Clark was not being completely honest with her, but his experience with Pete had made him wary of confiding in anyone. He just couldn't bear to lose Lana, too.

TORNADO!

When a tornado sent Lana and her truck flying off the road, Clark was there to rescue her as usual. Although Lana has often wondered about Clark's amazing knack of being in the right place at the right time, she has never guessed the truth about him.

At the time the tornado hit, Clark was at the Spring Formal and Lana was saying goodbye to Whitney as he left to join the military.

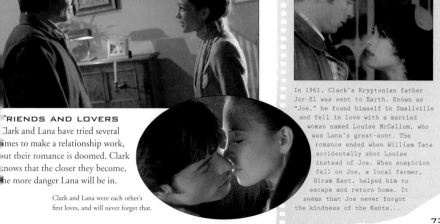

FRIENDS AND LOVERS

Clark and Lana have tried several times to make a relationship work, but their romance is doomed. Clark knows that the closer they become, the more danger Lana will be in.

Clark and Lana were each other's first loves, and will never forget that.

In 1961, Clark's Kryptonian father Jor-El was sent to Earth. Known as "Joe," he found himself in Smallville and fell in love with a married woman named Louise McCallum, who was Lana's great-aunt. The romance ended when William Tate accidentally shot Louise instead of Joe. When suspicion fell on Joe, a local farmer, Hiram Kent, helped him to escape and return home. It seems that Joe never forgot the kindness of the Kents...

CLARK'S FATHERS

Jonathan Kent and Jor-El had very different ideas on what is best for Clark/Kal-El. He may not have been Clark's biological father, but that never mattered to Jonathan. He loved his son and worked hard to give him a regular upbringing. However, Jor-El has other plans for his son. He believes that Kryptonians are higher beings, and has informed Clark that he is on Earth to conquer it.

Jonathan tried to instill strong morals into his son. Although he sometimes appeared strict, he always had his son's best interests at heart.

SELFLESS DAD

When Clark was in Metropolis under the influence of red kryptonite, a desperate Jonathan begged Jor-El for a means of bringing his son home. Jor-El agreed and temporarily gave Jonathan superpowers of his own. However, Jor-El acted on the understanding that one day Jonathan would deliver Clark to him.

Jonathan would have done anything to bring his son home, but the superpowers left him with a serious heart condition.

Two years later, following Jor-El's warning that someone close to Clark would die, Jonathan suffered a fatal heart attack.

Clark Kent truly became an adult after the death of the man he regarded as his real father. Despite Martha's reassurance, Clark felt that he was to blame for Jonathan's death. He would rather that he had died instead.

PAINFUL DESTINY

Jor-El first communicated with Clark through the ship that sent him to Earth. He told Clark that it was time to accept his destiny. He showed Clark visions of Jonathan, Martha, and Lana, and said that Clark's family and friends on Earth had served their purpose, and that it was time to leave them. Clark refused to listen to Jor-El, and insisted on creating his own destiny.

When Clark refused to obey him, Jor-El blasted him with a white light that branded his chest with a Kryptonian symbol. It served as a painful reminder that Jor-El was in control.

CALL ME JOE...

Years before he sent his son to Earth, Jor-El spent some time in Kansas, as a "test" by his own father, Seyg-El. During this time he called himself "Joe" and was helped by a kind farmer named Hiram Kent. Perhaps this later inspired him to send his son to Smallville, meaning that—as Martha always suspected—the Kents finding Clark was no accident.

JOR-EL'S HUMAN FORM

When Lionel's body was charged by a Kryptonian element, it became an oracle of Kryptonian knowledge and a vessel that Jor-El could use to communicate with Clark. In this form, Jor-El told Clark that the life force of someone he loves would be taken in exchange for his life.

Later, Jor-El would assist Clark and use Lionel's body to explain how to defeat General Zod.

MARTHA KENT

As she watched her son Clark make the difficult journey into adulthood, Martha Kent also approached new challenges in her own life. Not content to be just a farmer's wife, she eventually took over Lana's old job as manager of the Talon coffee shop, with the full support of her family. However, the sudden death of her husband has presented Martha with an even greater test—his position as a Kansas State senator. Even though she had some initial hesitations about filling her husband's shoes, she took the new job and now works to serve the state of Kansas and honor her husband's memory to the best to her ability.

PROUD PARENTS

Jonathan and Martha Kent watched proudly as their son graduated from Smallville High School. Unfortunately, the graduation ceremonies were interrupted by the second meteor shower, so many of Smallville's students were denied the opportunity of taking the momentous graduation walk. Clark had enrolled at Central Kansas University because he wanted to remain close to home so he would still be able to help his father on the farm. Although the Kents would never have asked him to make that sacrifice, they were proud of their son's sense of duty and honor.

At first, Martha wasn't sure that running for senator was the best idea for Jonathan or their family, but she never doubted that her husband could do a great job. As always, she gave Jonathan her full support and did everything she could to help his campaign.

SENATOR'S SHOCK DEATH

Newly elected Kansas senator Jonathan Kent died suddenly yesterday at his home in Smallville. He was 45 years old and had suffered from a serious heart condition for a number of years.

A simple farmer all his life, Kent swept to victory with a campaign founded on strong family values and support for state farmers.

"He really was one of a kind," Kent's predecessor, Jack Jennings said in a statement. Jennings, who was forced to step down following a political scandal last year, had been a close friend of Senator Kent for many years.

Lex Luthor, Kent's opponent in the senatorial campaign, also issued a statement. "It was a sad moment to learn the news of Jonathan Kent's passing," it said. "My deepest condolences go to the Kent family."

Jonathan Kent is survived by his wife Martha and son, Clark. A memorial service is planned for Thursday in Smallville.

Martha is a loving mom and always there for her son when he needs her. She would do anything to protect him and his secret, even if it means putting herself in danger. After his father's death, Clark needs his mom more than ever, and Martha is always ready to offer advice and support, despite her important role as senator.

As a state senator, Martha can finally put her law studies to good use. She relishes the challenge of carrying on her husband's noble work.

LIONEL'S OFFER
When Jonathan's political campaign was low on funds, Martha secretly accepted a donation from Lionel Luthor. Jonathan was very angry when he found out, but Martha was only thinking of him.

LEX & CLARK

Lex Luthor and Clark Kent seemed unlikely friends. Wealthy city boy Lex and humble farm boy Clark come from very different backgrounds and have little in common. However, when Clark rescued Lex from a watery grave, it was the start of a complex friendship. In Clark, Lex had finally found a friend who accepted him for who he was and saw him as much more than just the son of Lionel Luthor. In turn, Clark benefited from having an older confidant with more life experience. Within weeks of the rescue, Lex Luthor and Clark Kent were best friends.

When Clark heard piercing noises at Lex's wedding rehearsal dinner, Lex was genuinely concerned about him.

SECRET EXPOSED

When Lionel Luthor had Lex drugged to make everyone believe he was insane, Clark was there to help his friend. He was even forced to perform a superfeat right in front of Lex when Morgan Edge tried to run him down. Although Lex babbled that he knew the truth about Clark Kent, his mad ravings were ignored by everyone else.

Meeting the Kents, particularly Clark, showed Lex a set of values that he was deprived of while growing up with his father in Metropolis. For a short time, his desire for the Kents' acceptance and approval made Lex a better man.

When Lex was placed in the Belle Reve asylum, his memories of this experience were wiped.

Acting on a tip from Lionel Luthor, Clark discovered that Lex had a secret room all about him. Clark's extraordinary luck and the events surrounding their first meeting were still a mystery to Lex, and he was determined to uncover the truth about his friend. After Clark's discovery, the room was supposedly dismantled, but Clark would never trust Lex in the same way again.

Lex and Clark found their friendship becoming increasingly strained, and as time passed, their differences in character became more apparent. Even Shelby, the Kent's dog took an instant dislike to the younger Luthor, which did not escape Clark's notice.

TEAMWORK

Although their friendship had been strained beyond repair by this point, Clark and Lex were forced to work together when Lionel Luthor and Martha Kent were both taken captive by a tormentor who threatened to kill them.

LEX AND CLARK FACTS

• Rachel Dunleavy thought that Clark was her long-lost son Lucas. Lex was particularly delighted at the idea that he and Clark could be half-brothers.

• Lex employed rogue journalist Roger Nixon to find the truth about Clark's rescue of him. When Nixon attempted to kill Jonathan Kent, Lex shot and killed him instead.

In many ways, Lex was the older brother that Clark never had. In fact, when Lex introduced Clark to his newly-discovered brother Lucas, Clark was a little jealous. However, Clark has come to realize that he and Lex are worlds apart.

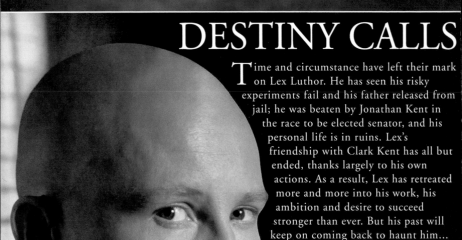

DESTINY CALLS

Time and circumstance have left their mark on Lex Luthor. He has seen his risky experiments fail and his father released from jail; he was beaten by Jonathan Kent in the race to be elected senator, and his personal life is in ruins. Lex's friendship with Clark Kent has all but ended, thanks largely to his own actions. As a result, Lex has retreated more and more into his work, his ambition and desire to succeed stronger than ever. But his past will keep on coming back to haunt him...

Lex's thirst for knowledge and his will to win are unstoppable. Like his father, Lex has learned that he must be ruthless to get what he wants. Though Lex still intends to do good, he may not be able to escape his destiny.

PARANOID?

Lex Luthor had experienced so many break-ins and attempts on his life inside his own mansion that he installed a secure Panic Room beside his study. Does he really have that many crazed enemies, or has his paranoia reached a new level?

THE REAL LEX?

An experiment with black kryptonite split Lex in two. The dark side "Alexander" tried to kill Clark and Chloe, kissed and then evicted a shocked Lana, and locked the good Lex in the cellar. When the two Lexes merged again, the question remained—which was the real Lex?

When elderly blind woman Cassandra Carver saw a vision of Lex's future, it showed him as president of the United States in an apocalyptic world where blood poured from the sky. The shock of the terrible vision killed Cassandra before she could share it with Lex.

LEX LUTHOR SHOT

Senatorial candidate and LuthorCorp heir, Alexander "Lex" Luthor was seriously ill in the hospital last night following an attempted carjacking. Lex, son of billionaire Lionel Luthor, was shot during the incident and is said to be in critical but stable condition.

Mr. Luthor was immediately rushed to the Davis Clinic in Metropolis for

emergency surgery. The young senatorial hopeful remained comatose for several hours with his close friend Lana Lang by his side before his condition eventually stabilized. Mr Luthor's surgeon, Dr. Tom Litvack, expects his patient to make a full recovery.

> "Despite this setback, the Luthor campaign is determined to march on."

One arrest has been made in connection with the incident. The Luthor camp has pledged to continue campaigning as normal.

FRIENDS TO ENEMIES
Lex and Clark were once as close as brothers, but Lex's desire to uncover the truth about Clark, and his often ruthless behavior, have driven them apart. Over the years Clark's friendship has been tested to its limits, and he feels that he can no longer trust his one-time best friend.

ARTHUR CURRY

AC made his first splash in Smallville saving Lois after she hit her head during a botched dive.

Like Clark Kent, Arthur "AC" Curry has yet to discover the true extent of his abilities. He has enhanced powers underwater and cannot survive for long periods of time without water. It is believed that AC was born with these powers—they are certainly not meteor-based, as he had never previously visited Smallville. AC is committed to doing everything he can to protect all the creatures of the sea. His environmental concerns often require a proactive approach that some might consider to be only a little short of eco-terrorism!

A DAY AT THE BEACH

When Chloe and Lois joined Clark and Lana for a relaxing day at Crater Lake, they were not expecting to meet a handsome blond stranger. But of course, with Lois Lane around it was never going to be quiet day…

ARTHUR CURRY FACTS

- According to official records, Arthur Curry was born and raised in southern Florida.

- He is a sophomore at the University of Miami, a major in Marine Biology, and has won several college swimming competitions.

- AC has a criminal record after breaking in to the Ocean Village Resort, and releasing eight dolphins back into the ocean.

LEVIATHAN

AC broke into an underground LuthorCorp facility to destroy a project Lex was developing, a high-tech sonar weapon known as *Leviathan*. *Leviathan* emits a focused soundwave that can tear a submarine in half, and also kills all marine life in its path.

When Lex Luthor realized that AC needed water to survive, he tormented him by keeping it just out of his reach. His strength seriously depleted by the lack of water, AC was powerless to fight back.

After saying farewell to Lois, AC swam off into the sunset. His desire to protect the ocean and all the creatures in it will keep him busy. Some people in Florida are already talking of a mysterious "Aquaman." If LuthorCorp begins using underwater weapons that threaten that environment, Lex Luthor can count on meeting AC again.

Lois was hugely attracted to the man who saved her life, and wondered if she might perhaps have a latent interest in do-gooders. In Lois, AC found one of his first true friends since beginning his environmental crusade. Unfortunately, their romance had no future as AC had places to go beyond Smallville.

Although their methods clashed, Clark realized the danger of Lex's *Leviathan* weapon and he assisted AC in sabotaging it. Clark was beginning to understand that his "friend" Lex had a dark side...

83

BRAINIAC

The spilling of Genevieve Teague's blood on the Air element summoned the Brain Inter-Active Construct (Brainiac) from outer space. This advanced Kryptonian computer was created by Jor-El, but corrupted by General Zod. Taking the form of a spacecraft, it also contained two Kryptonian criminals, Nam-Ek and Aethyr. Once on Earth, Brainiac assumed the identity of Central Kansas University professor Milton Fine. Its mission was to secure Zod's release from the Phantom Zone.

Brainiac had the ability to alter its form and control other computers. As Fine it had all the powers of a being from the planet Krypton. Its intelligence was unmatched, and it was programmed with several scenarios in which to achieve Zod's goals.

BRAINIAC FACTS

• Brainiac had the ability to appear as multiple Milton Fine bodies simultaneously.

• When Fine was impaled in the Fortress of Solitude, he seemed to die, but in reality Brainiac was infecting the Fortress's infrastructure. Brainiac then regenerated into a new Fine body and was next seen in Honduras.

• Lex Luthor kept tabs in Fine's whereabouts through his contacts in Project Mercury.

• When Brainiac managed to take over all of the electronic systems in Metropolis, it caused chaos and mayhem throughout the city.

PROFESSOR FINE

Brainiac's first plan was to assimilate himself into Clark Kent's life. He took the form of one of Clark's

Professor Fine asked Clark how he would affect the world for generations to come.

professors at Central Kansas University and then offered Clark a job as his research assistant. This gave Brainiac the ideal opportunity to learn how to manipulate Kal-El.

THE SHIP

The mysterious spaceship that arrived with the second meteor shower was actually Brainiac's true form.

Brainiac arranged for Clark Kent to be infected by a splinter of silver kryptonite which made him paranoid. Brainiac then appeared to save Clark, leading him to believe that he was a fellow Kryptonian and thereby gaining his trust.

Silver kryptonite results in paranoid behavior and delusions.

TEAMING UP

When Lex Luthor located Brainiac in Honduras, he agreed to help him create a super-virus. Lex believed that doing so would create the ultimate vaccine, but Brainiac planned to use it to turn Lex into Zod's vessel.

LEX & LANA

When Lex Luthor first got to know Lana Lang she was a high school student and the object of his best friend's affection. Lex often gave Clark advice about Lana, but over the years Lex found himself becoming attracted to her. As Lana grew into a smart and beautiful woman, she and Lex became friends and then business partners. For her part, Lana liked the fact that Lex—unlike Clark— seemed willing to share his entire life with her, without any secrets. Lex also appealed to the side of Lana that had always longed for something more than Smallville had to offer.

When the old Talon movie theater was about to be sold, Lana convinced Lex to become a business partner and turn it into Smallville's hottest coffee shop and meeting place.

SHARED CURIOSITY
Lex and Lana bonded further when they joined forces to find out more about the spaceship that crashed in Smallville during the second meteor shower. This shared interest, combined with their changing relationships with Clark, brought them closer than ever and laid the foundation for the next stage of their friendship.

WHAT IF...

As Lex faced death, he had a vision of what his life could have been like. In his dream, Lex had given up his wealth and was happily married to Lana. However, in the dream Lana died while giving birth to their second child, and Lex was powerless to save her.

GETTING CLOSER

After Lana's breakup with Clark, she and Lex both tried to deny that they were anything more than friends. However, when Lana impulsively kissed Lex, they could no longer hide their true feelings for one another. Despite warnings from Lois and Chloe, Lex and Lana were happy. Concerned about the situation and knowing that Lex could not be trusted, Clark tried his best to avoid them both.

Lex's honesty brought him and Lana closer than ever.

PANIC ROOM

Rogue policemen entered the Luthor mansion demanding answers about the Kryptonian ship. They shot Lex, who escaped to his Panic Room with Lana. A delirious Lex told Lana about his dream, and how she was the best part of it. He also told her everything he knew about the ship.

DEVELOPING POWERS

As Clark has grown older, he has discovered more new and amazing powers. Some abilities, such as flight, have been brought on by the influence of red kryptonite, other new abilities, such as superhearing, have developed naturally. Clark has no way of knowing if he has reached his full potential already, or if he will keep on developing even more superpowers in the future.

LEAPING TALL BUILDINGS

When Lionel Luthor and Martha Kent were held hostage in the LuthorCorp Plaza, Clark had to make a giant leap from a neighboring building to rescue them. This new-found ability to leap tall buildings in a single bound surprised even Clark, especially as he was afraid of heights!

INVULNERABLE

Clark has long been aware that he is virtually impervious to harm, but his body is getting stronger and tougher all the time. These days he can stop an oncoming car traveling at full speed. While the car won't look too great afterward, Clark will barely have a scratch!

The first few times that Clark was shot, he was left with a little bruising, but as he has gotten stronger, bullets just bounce right off him without leaving a mark. Thanks to his superspeed, he can also catch bullets in mid-air before they hit him, or anyone else.

FIREPROOF

Clark can withstand extremely high temperatures and fire. When some kryptonite-inhaling bullies left him to die in a burning building, Clark emerged unscathed, with only his clothing slightly singed!

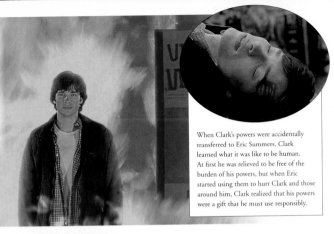

When Clark's powers were accidentally transferred to Eric Summers, Clark learned what it was like to be human. At first he was relieved to be free of the burden of his powers, but when Eric started using them to hurt Clark and those around him, Clark realized that his powers were a gift that he must use responsibly.

SUPERHEARING

Clark was temporarily blinded by sonic-screaming meteor freak Nathan Dean as he tried to foil a jewelry store robbery. The piercing sound, combined with the sudden loss of vision, awakened a new power in Clark—superhearing. Now Clark can use this power to overhear important conversations or cries for help from miles away.

FLIGHT

Clark Kent has not yet mastered the ability to fly, but it seems that he does have the power. When Jor-El turned Clark into Kal, he was able to fly through the air at supersonic speeds. When Kal reverted back to being Clark, he could not recall this ability. It remains to be seen if Clark Kent will ever fly.

THE FUTURE

Clark Kent's journey so far has taken him from Krypton to Smallville, and from a shy, clumsy Kansas farm boy to a grown man who is only just beginning to understand his superpowers and his extraordinary destiny. As a college student, Clark faces new challenges every day, but he has also learned some valuable lessons outside of school—most significantly that not all friends can be trusted, and that there are others on Earth with potentially more power than him.

Now that his father's deadliest foe, Zod, has been unleashed and his power given to Lex Luthor, Clark faces decisions that will lead him to a destiny far beyond Smallville.

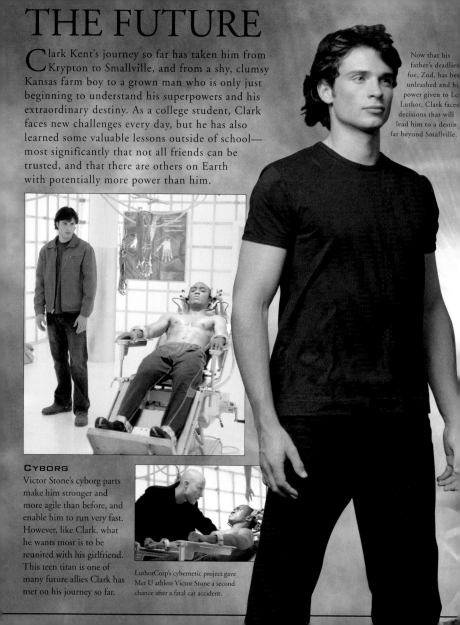

CYBORG

Victor Stone's cyborg parts make him stronger and more agile than before, and enable him to run very fast. However, like Clark, what he wants most is to be reunited with his girlfriend. This teen titan is one of many future allies Clark has met on his journey so far.

LuthorCorp's cybernetic project gave Met U athlete Victor Stone a second chance after a fatal car accident.

MASTER PLAN

Months after Clark Kent thought him dead, Milton Fine was seen in a plague-ridden part of Honduras, collecting viruses for his latest scheme. Joining forces with Lex Luthor, Brainiac was able to unleash massive chaos, and Clark was virtually powerless to stop it.

ex has been open with na about his plans th Fine and vows use his powers to ve her the world, either of them are vare that Lex is lly Zod's vessel.

ANGEL OF VENGEANCE

By day Andrea Rojas wears a pair of glasses and pretends to be a bumbling reporter, but at night she is the crime-fighting vigilante Angel of Vengeance. Her disguise has given Clark an idea...

When Simone, an hypnotic seductress, used her meteor-enhanced necklace on Clark, it made him want to kill Lex Luthor. Only Chloe's quick thinking saved Lex.

This time around, Clark Kent was the one who needed saving! To break the spell, Chloe exposed Clark to green kryptonite.

CLARK'S DESTINY?

When meteor freak Jordan Cross touched Clark, instead of seeing the moment of his death, he saw a flowing red cape flying through space. What does this image mean? Will Clark live forever? One thing is certain, Smallville is not the end of Clark Kent's journey...

SEASON SIX

Clark Kent escaped the Phantom Zone only to face new challenges at home. His departure released some of the Zone's worst prisoners, and it became Clark's job to stop them. New allies arrived in the form of Green Arrow and John Jones, and old allies Bart Allen, Arthur Curry, and Victor Stone returned. Clark also had to learn to live in a world where Lana Lang had left him for his sworn enemy, Lex Luthor.

GREEN ARROW

To the uninitiated, Oliver Queen may have appeared to be a carefree playboy, but by night, Oliver took on the mantle of the Green Arrow— a brilliant archer who took from the rich and returned to the poor. Disguised as the Emerald Archer, Queen was determined to rid the streets of Metropolis of crime.

OLIVER AND LOIS

Despite a first meeting full of misunderstandings, Lois Lane and Oliver Queen had instant chemistry. Lois Lane had no idea that when she wrote about "the Green Arrow Bandit" that the vigilante was in fact her own boyfriend.

While Oliver admired Clark, and in some ways was even jealous of his abilities, he felt that Clark should be more proactive, particularly when dealing with evils such as Level 33.1.

CHLOE AND JIMMY

Chloe Sullivan finally found love with young photographer Jimmy Olsen. They first met when Chloe was an intern at the *Daily Planet* and rekindled their romance when the met up again. However, Chloe still had some lingering feelings for Clark Kent.

Chloe and Jimmy were reunited during the events of Black Thursday.

MANHUNTER

John Jones became one of Clark's most unexpected allies in the fight against his enemies from the Phantom Zone. He stopped the Zone escapee Aldar before the villain seriously injured Clark, and later helped stop a Zoner who was actually inside Clark's brain.

LEX AND LANA

Lex and Lana grew increasingly close, and at one time it even seemed like they were going to be parents. The Luthor-Lang drama would bring a wedding, a lot of lies, and the ultimate betrayal. Maybe Lana Lang has not quite gotten over Clark Kent...

HEROES UNITED

Oliver Queen united a currently unnamed group that included Aquaman (Arthur Curry), Impulse (Bart Allen), Cyborg (Victor Stone), and of course the Green Arrow to take down several of LuthorCorp's facilities. Clark was invited to join their group, but turned down the offer because his first priority was to track down the remaining Phantom Zone escapees.

THE ULTIMATE REFERENCE

THE DC COMICS ENCYCLOPEDIA

Packed with information and thrilling comic book art from the world's leading comic book publisher, this definitive one-volume encyclopedia features over 1,000 classic DC Comics characters, including SUPERMAN, BATMAN, WONDER WOMAN, THE JOKER, and CATWOMAN! All of the world-famous super heroes and super-villains are here, as well as a host of lesser-known weird, wild, and wonderful characters. Illustrated with spectacular images from the original comic books, the drama and excitement of more than 60 years of comic book history explodes off of every page!

FOR THE ULTIMATE FAN

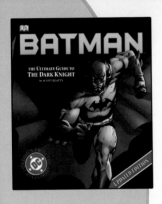

BATMAN: THE ULTIMATE GUIDE TO THE DARK KNIGHT

Given unparalleled access to the DC archives, DK presents an in-depth look at BATMAN'S crime-fighting career, his allies and his foes, illustrated with artwork from the original comic books.

TM & © 2007 DC Comics.

SUPERMAN: THE ULTIMATE GUIDE TO THE MAN OF STEEL

This celebration of the superpowered MAN OF STEEL contains full details of his thrilling adventures and the unforgettable cast of characters he has encountered, illustrated with stunning images from the original comics.

TM & © 2007 DC Comics.

FOR MORE DC COMICS TITLES, VISIT HTTP://US.DK.COM/POPCULTURE

LONDON, NEW YORK, MUNICH,
MELBOURNE, and DELHI

Designers	Lauren Egan, Jon Hall & Dan Bunyan
Senior Editor	Catherine Saunders
Publishing Manager	Simon Beecroft
Brand Manager	Rob Perry
Category Publisher	Alex Allan
DTP Designer	Hanna Ländin
Production	Rochelle Talary

This American Edition, 2007
First American Edition, 2006
Published in the United States by
DK Publishing, Inc., 375 Hudson Street
New York, New York 10014
06 07 08 10 9 8 7 6 5 4 3 2 1

Published in Great Britain by Dorling Kindersley Limited.

A catalog record for this book is available from the Library of Congress.

DK books are available at special discounts for bulk purchases for sales promotions, premiums,
fund-raising, or educational use. For details, contact: DK Publishing Special Markets,
375 Hudson Street, New York, NY 10014
SpecialSales@dk.com

ISBN-13 978-0-75663-530-5

Color reproduction by Media Development and Printing Ltd, UK

Printed and bound by Lake Book Manufacturing, Inc., USA

ACKNOWLEDGMENTS
Dorling Kindersley would like to thank:
Al Gough and Miles Millar, the cast and crew of *Smallville*, Mark Warshaw, Christopher Freyer,
Neil Sadhu, Chris Cerasi, Susan Kesser, Nia Figueroa, and Craig Byrne.

Visit DC Comics online at www.dccomics.com
or at keyword DC Comics on America Online

Discover more at
www.dk.com